CHANSON DADA

CHANSON DADA

DADA

TRANSLATED BY LEE HARWOOD

TRISTAN TZARA
SELECTED POEMS

BLACK
WIDOW
PRESS

Boston, Mass.

CHANSON DADA
TRISTAN TZARA, SELECTED POEMS

English language translations copyright © Lee Harwood 1987, 2005
These translations of Tristan Tzara's works were originally made with the permission of Christophe Tzara.
Tristan Tzara: Oeuvres Complètes, © Flammarion, Paris (1975–1982).
Excerpt from *L'homme approximatif* (1925–1930), © Editions Gallimard, Paris, 1968.
Cover photo: Tristan Tzara, 1917; photographer unknown.
Marcel Duchamp, *Fountain*, 1917/1964, photo credit: CNAC/MNAM/Dist. Réunion des Musées Nationaux / Art Resource, NY.

    Black Widow Press is an imprint of Commonwealth Books, Inc., Boston, MA. Distributed to the trade by NBN (National Book Network) throughout North America, Canada, and the U.K. All Black Widow Press books are printed on acid-free paper, and glued into bindings. Black Widow Press and its logo are registered trademarks of Commonwealth Books, Inc.

Joseph S. Phillips and Susan J. Wood, Ph.D., Publishers
www.blackwidowpress.com

ISBN-13: 978-0-9768449-0-7
ISBN-10: 0-9768449-0-7

Library of Congress Control Number: 2005905003

        Library of Congress Cataloging-in-Publication Data

Tzara, Tristan, 1896-1963.
  [Poems. English. Selections]
  Chanson Dada : Tristan Tzara, selected poems / translated by Lee Harwood.
      p. cm.
  Includes bibliographical references.
  ISBN-13: 978-0-9768449-0-7 (trade : alk. paper)
  ISBN-10: 0-9768449-0-7 (trade : alk. paper)
  1. Tzara, Tristan, 1896–1963—Translations into English. I. Harwood, Lee. II. Title.

PQ2639.Z3A25 2005
841'.912--dc22

                                                                2005027655

Printed in the United States

10 9 8 7 6 5 4 3 2

In memory of Gael Turnbull
(1928–2004)
poet explorer

Tristan Tzara personally approved the publication of a number of these translations and his son Christophe Tzara later gave his permission to publish this selection of his father's poems. My whole-hearted thanks for their kindness and generosity. I would also like to thank Michel Couturier for his advice on my translations.

Lee Harwood

This second edition printed in memory of Lee Harwood
(1919–2015)

Foreword

'The individual... lives poetry every moment that he affirms his existence. The poetic image itself, as much as experience, is not only a product of reason and imagination, it is valid only if it has been lived. Every creation is therefore, for the poet, an aggressive affirmation of his consciousness.' Tristan Tzara wrote this manifesto for his *Dialectics of Poetry* in 1946 soon after the 'Second World War' had left Europe and European culture in ruins. It is no exaggeration to say that Tzara's entire life was as varied, wide ranging and energetic as this statement, though no such statement of belief could possibly reveal the magic, the force, the irony and wit, the essential humanist insistence and open emotion to be found in his poems. The poems speak so clearly for themselves that they need no explanation.

Tristan Tzara was a writer for whom artistic and political revolution were one and the same. These qualities permeate all his work with its continual opposition to traditionalism in all its repressive forms, whether moral or aesthetic. He was a poet, a playwright, a prose writer and an instigator. He was also a critic who wrote and lectured widely on art and literature, an editor and a scholar. A man of immense vigour, he continually moved forward throughout his life. In his time he published thirty-seven volumes of poetry and prose-poetry, five plays, six collections of literary and art criticism, and a volume of manifestoes. This list doesn't include the many reprints of his books and numerous contributions to magazines. There were also all the articles and prefaces to exhibition catalogues that he wrote on his artist contemporaries. In turn Tzara's active concern for modern art was equally reciprocated by these artists in their many collaborations with him. His own books were illustrated by Hans Arp, Georges Braque, Salvador Dali, Sonia Delaunay, Max Ernst, Alberto Giacometti, Juan Gris, Marcel Janco, Vassily Kandinsky, Paul Klee, Fernand Léger, André Masson, Henri Matisse, Joan Miró, Francis Picabia, Pablo Picasso, Man Ray, and Yves Tanguy.

Tristan Tzara was born Samuel Rosenstock on 16th April 1896 in the small town of Moinesti in eastern Romania. His parents were wealthy Jewish merchants. He went to school in Moinesti and then Bucharest, and from 1914 to 1915 attended the university in Bucharest to study mathematics and philosophy. His career as a poet started early. By his late teens he had already been writing for some time, founded the magazine *Simbolul* in 1912 with Ion Vinea and Marcel Janco, and had poems published in other magazines. These early Romanian poems were first signed 'S. Samyro', then 'Tristan', then 'Tzara', and eventually in 1915 the name of 'Tristan Tzara' was born in the magazine *Chemarea* edited by Tzara and Vinea.

In the autumn of 1915 his parents sent him to continue his studies at the university in Zurich. And it was in Zurich that he came to meet the future 'members' of the Dada movement, and to write exclusively in French. It would be nearly impossible to summarize all the Dada events. They were so many and so varied, and Tzara was almost always at the centre of them as one of the chief instigators and organizers. The list would have to begin with the first performance by the Dada group in the Cabaret Voltaire on 5th February 1916. This first event involved Hugo Ball, Emmy Hennings, Hans Arp, Marcel Janco, and Tzara. The cabaret was then to be followed by the discovery of the word Dada three days later when Tzara, Arp and Huelsenbeck randomly slid a paper-knife into the Larousse dictionary in search of a name for their new 'movement' or, rather, 'anti-movement.' (A fuller account of these events is to be found in my essay on Dada. See pages 113–140.)

But what is more relevant and revealing than such a list of Dada events is the cause of these events. The cause that inevitably shadowed and shaped their activities and art was the fact of the 1914–18 'Great War,' the 'First World War'. This was what drove Tzara and his companions to act as they did. As Hugo Ball wrote, the Dadaists were 'fighting against the agony of the times and against an inebriation with death.'[1] Their protests and creations were primarily an expression of this. The actions of the Dadaists—with their attacks on all that was considered 'reasonable' and 'true art', their anarchic mix of wild performance pieces and manifestos, disjointed music, collaged pictures, cut-up poems, African chants and random texts—were the one sane reaction any artist could have in a world apparently gone insane. As Tzara later wrote: 'We proclaimed our disgust... This war was not our war.... Dada was born from an urgent moral need, from an implacable desire to attain a moral absolute, from the deep feeling that man, at the centre of all creations of the spirit, must affirm his supremacy over notions emptied of all human substance, over dead objects and ill-gotten gains... Honour, Morality, Family, Art, Religion, Liberty, Fraternity, I don't know what, all these notions had once answered to human needs, now nothing remained of them but a skeleton of conventions, they had been divested of their initial content.'[2]

Inevitably bound to this moral concern was Tzara's insistence that words and actions should be the same, that value should again be returned to a language emptied of content, and that poetry itself should create a permanent atmosphere of openness and active change. His belief in poetry as an essential catalyst in society was to dominate all of Tzara's work. In his poetry he continually explored the frontiers of language and thought, continually pushed to the limits the possibilities of words, of what language might be able to reveal and convey. His moral and artistic concern was the very opposite of plodding social realism. Rather he trusted in the intelligence of his reader and the necessity of using language beyond any logical limits to reach those human realities and knowledges we are all aware of but can't clearly explain. As he said: 'To experience the effects, the reader must not wait until they are brought to him on a plate. Poetry must arouse in him an activity corresponding to the writer's. The reader must battle to conquer the sense and content. He must re-create the poetry to his own image. Poetry is an object to be conquered, all passivity before it leads only to deception.'[3]

During Tzara's time in Zurich he and the Dada group, through letters and publications such as Tzara's magazine *Dada*, built up links with an international avant-garde that shared some of their obsessions. Tzara was in contact with Apollinaire, Max Jacob and Pierre Reverdy in France, de Chirico and others in Italy, Raoul Hausmann and others in Germany, and Francis Picabia wherever he might be. With the end of the war and the reopening of frontiers the movement blossomed as its contacts widened, even though its initial cause had ceased.

At the beginning of 1920 Tzara went to Paris partly at the urging of André Breton and the *Littérature* group. He enrolled at the Faculté des Sciences to study chemistry, and then once more became intensely involved in all the Paris Dada events, writing, editing, lecturing, and, most of all, performing. The next three years were packed with such provocative activities, but, as Tzara later said, 'It lay in the very nature of Dada to put a term to its existence.'[2]

By 1922–23 the movement began to break up. One of the obvious reasons was the personal rivalry over leadership and approach that developed between André Breton and Tzara. This divided the group and culminated in a brawl at a performance of Tzara's play *Le coeur à gaz* in July 1923. But a truer reason was the fact that a protest movement can become stagnant, repeating tried formulas and provocations, and so lose its vitality. As circumstances change so must new ways be developed to tackle them.

After the death of Dada Tzara continued his own literary life in Paris, but avoided joining Breton's official Surrealist group in 1924. In 1925 he married the Swedish poet and painter Greta Knutson, and in 1927 they had a son, Christophe Tzara. It wasn't until 1929 that Tzara joined the Surrealists, by which time the group's character had altered to a more directly political one. He remained one of the prominent Surrealists until 1935. His long poem *L'homme approximatif,* written 1925–30, has been judged the poetic masterpiece of Surrealism. But alongside Tzara's great interest in surrealist approaches was his interest in Marxism since the late 1920s. Within the world of French Communism such a 'marriage'—Tzara's experimental book on dreams, *Grains et issues,* and his revolutionary concern—was not at all unusual nor inconsistent. His 1929 visit to Russia followed a well-worn path taken by French intellectuals of the period.

In 1935 Tzara finally broke with the Surrealists and gave his full attention and sympathy to the socialist-communist movement along with Louis Aragon, René Char, René Crevel, and later Paul Eluard. (It wasn't, though, until 1947 that he became a Communist Party member.) Such an allegiance saw its practical application not only in Tzara's writings but also in his activities during the Spanish Civil War. In 1936 Tzara and Christian Zervos compiled in Barcelona a catalogue of the art treasures of Catalonia for the Catalan Government, and Tzara himself helped get many of these treasures to safety. In 1937 he was secretary to the Committee for the Defence of Spanish Culture and organized the second international writers' congress in Madrid and Valencia. It was at this same time that Tzara's marriage broke up, and he and his wife were eventually divorced in 1942.

With the coming of the 'Second World War' and the German occupation of France, 1940–44, Tzara, unlike many 'revolutionary artists', stayed on and was an active member of the Resistance. With false papers he lived in Souillac from 1942–44, and was all the time involved in editing and publishing clandestine magazines, as well as helping in the Restistance. In the last year of the war Tzara held various official posts in the French propaganda service and was president of the Centre des Intellectuels in Toulouse. It was also in 1945 that he helped found the Institut d'Etudes Occitanes in Toulouse.

In 1946 Tzara once more returned to an energetic literary life. In this year he had five books of poems published. He also wrote, lectured, and travelled throughout Europe to attend writers' conferences. For the rest of his life Tzara followed this vigorous and restless pattern. As well as his own writing he published essays on poetry, did extensive research on the work of Villon and Rabelais, wrote on Picasso and other painters such as Rousseau and Bracelli, and prefaced the collected works of Rimbaud, Villon, and Tristan Corbiere, and collections of Nazim Hikmet and Guillaume Apollinaire. He even wrote a text to accompany a series of photographs of contemporary Egypt. In the year before his death he was in Africa to attend a conference in Salisbury on African art—a subject that had fascinated him all his life, and which he had collected and written about for many years.

The experience of the war and the bleakness of the post-war years in Europe marked his late poems with a certain bitterness. But though the poems are bitter and a far cry from the earlier exuberance of his Dada and surrealist writings they are never resigned nor totally pessimistic. Rather they affirm Tzara's statement: 'I do not believe in an earthly paradise. For at every stage of human evolution everything once again becomes an object to be overcome. The individual affirms himself in the struggle, by the struggle. You must have passed through the depths to reach a certain height. You must have risked your life, been close to death to attain consciousness. Have staked all you have to win everything there is in this struggle for existence which is the affirmation of the self. And never a pause, never any ultimate peace, otherwise everything falls asleep around you and life crumbles away, becomes a form of wretched matter that consumes and annuls itself.'[2] It is this insistence more than any other that summarizes Tzara's work and life.

On December 24th, 1963, he died in Paris of lung cancer at the age of sixty-seven.

NOTES:

1 Hugo Ball, *Flucht aus der Zeit* (1927).
2 Tristan Tzara, *Le Surréalisme et l'après-guerre* (1947).
3 Tristan Tzara, *La Dialectique de la poésie* (1946–47) (included in notes to *Le Surréalisme et l'après-guerre* collection).

Contents

The Translations

The poems in this selection are arranged as near as is possible in the chronological order of their dates of composition.

—Lee Harwood

evening

fishermen return with the waters' stars
they share bread with the poor
thread beads for the blind
emperors go out in the park at this hour which
is like the bitterness of engravings

servants bathe the hunting dogs
the light puts on gloves
shut window in consequence
go out room light like the apricot's stone
like the church's priest

good lord: make soft wool for doleful lovers
paint the little birds in ink and renew the face
of the moon

—let's go catch beetles
to shut them in the box
—let's go to the streams
to make baked earth jugs
— let's hug ourselves
by the fountain
—let's go to the public park
until the cock crows
and the town is scandalized
or to the loft
the hay prickles you hear the cows low
then they remember the little ones
let's go

Cosmic Realities Vanilla Tobacco Dawnings

1

listen I'm going to make a poem but don't laugh
four roads surround us and we tell them light
ON THE PRAYER POSTS AND YOU WERE TALKING TO
elephants at the circus like the light
I don't want you to be sick anymore you know
but why why do you want to whistle this morning
telephone
I don't want I don't want and he grips me TOO
TOO HARD

2

this copper morning
your voice trembles on the line
yellow locked itself in the villa like blood
the woman covered in verdigris of verdigris
dissolved like mist in small bells
tear—seaman's ticket—white tear
here's a light which could be black
flower

3

on steel and salt lilies tell me again that your
mother was kind

4

I am a line which expands and I want to grow in an
iron tin pipe
I say that to amuse you

5

not because I could have been a wax archangel
or evening rain or car catalogue

6

in the graves red life is boiling
for silence I'll have my joys
you told me that I may pity you
and I didn't cry when you saw me, but I would have liked
to cry in the tramway
you said to me I want to leave
the pearls of the tower of my throat were cold drum-major
for the hearts and slide
insects in the thought don't bite me,

ah ⎰ flower of fingers
   ⎱ the water snarls

and if you like I'll laugh like a drain and like a
fire

7

say: empty thought
quick you know
I'll be a
cello

8

I'll hold your coat for you when you leave as if you weren't
my sister

9

peals
in frost steel
do you sleep when it rains?

10

the farm hands wash the hunting dogs
and the king strolls followed by the judges who resemble
doves
I've seen at the sea's edge the tower bound with its sad
PRISONER
in the pits switch on
in consequence
lord lord   }   of ice
forgive me

11

LARGE TEARS slide the length of the draperies
head of horses on the basalt like
glass toys between the stars with chains
for the animals
and in the glaciers I would like to follow
with root
with my sickness
with the sand that swarms in my brain
for I am very intelligent
and with the darkness

12

THE PORCELAIN song thought
I'm tired—the song of queens
the tree bursts with food like a lamp
I CRY want to rise higher than the fountain snake
in the sky for earthly gravity no longer exists at school and in
the brain
my hand is cold and dry but it has caressed the spurt
of water
and I have again seen something in the sky as the water screws
the fruits and the gum

13

but I am serious in thinking about what's happened to me
lila
LILA
LILA
LILA
LILA
your brother shouts
you tell him
between the leaves of the book your hand
moist
with lime paint my belief
burns without light in the wire
LILA

14

your eye is large
lord in the draperies
your eye runs behind me
your eye is large as a ship forgive me
send medicines
the stone

14(a)

lover's heart open in the stream and electricity
let's consider the point
always the same
hairs grow around it
it begins to jump
grow
climb towards the final burst
encircle slips
quickly
quickly
rolling
nocturnal
turnings

15

among the sorrows there are organisms and the rain
your fingers TURNINGS

16

bay
your heart will fly making things so high
in flights of shudders squeezed like the tree
between the blushes of splendours
you leave
the paths
the branches
lick the snow of thighs

17

where one sees bridges connect breaths in the night
the darkness divides and collects in the villas
led by paths and winds towards your caress
rain

18

the horse eats coloured snakes
be quiet!

19

the stone
dances dances lord
the fever thinks a flower
dances dances on the hot stone
tress
discordantly begins again for the darkness my sister, my sister?

The Dada Review

five negresses in a car
have exploded following the five directions of my fingers
when sometimes I place my hand on my breast to pray to god
there's a damp light of old moon birds around my head
the green halo of saints lifted from mental escapes
tralalalalalalalalalalalalala
that you now see burst in the shells

somewhere there's a young man who eats his lungs
he farted so brilliantly that the house became midnight
like a return of birds that's sung about in poems
and death bursting from cannons stops the conversation of vultures
the very large sailingboat opens its book like an angel however
your leaves spring are stuck a fine page of typography
zoumbai zoumbai zoumbai di
I've dealt with all good and evil ah the joy of the general
there's why I put a shroud on each heart and on
each shroud there is our lord and on each lord
there is my heart
my heart I've given it a tip heehee

The Jugglers

the brains swell collapse
        heavy balloons are drained collapse
               (the ventriloquist's words)
swell collapse swell collapse
        collapse
                dissolved organs
the clouds also have these shapes now and then
               the widows get bored watching them
                    now and then
      listen to the vertigo
         number acrobatics
         in the mathematician's head
    NTOUCA who leaps
           jester's cap and bells
who is dada who is DADA
      the static poem is a new invention
MBOCO the asthmatic   HwS2
   10054   moumbimba
   there's a machine
   machine
      the vowels are white blood cells
   the vowels lengthen
       lengthen   we gnaw clock
               are clasped
AND THERE A LIGHT RUNS ALONG THE ROPES
      smoke issues from the tight-rope walker's head
my aunt is crouching on the trapeze in the gymnasium
      her tits are herring's heads
        she has fins
      and pulls pulls pulls her breast's accordion
she pulls pulls pulls pulls her breast's accordion glwawawa
prohabab

in the small towns the sun smoulders under the ploughs in front of
the inn
                    nf nf nf tatai
the small boys fart watching the circus's luggage
where there are lice
and grandmothers covered in soft tumours
that is to say in polypi

The Seaman

he makes love with a one-legged woman
the narrowness of a pondichéry ring
her belly which grinds greegree is opened

where the low and oblong animals leave
in your interior there are smoking lamps
the swamp of blue honey
crouching cat in the gold of a flemish tavern
boom boom
lots of sand yellow cyclist
'châteauneuf des papes'
manhattan there are buckets of shit in front of you
mbaze mbaze bazebaze mleganga garoo
you flow quickly into me
kangaroos in the boat's entrails
wait I'm first going to put my impressions in order
the seated trippers lace at the water's edge
thrust your fingers in the sockets so that the light bursts like grenades
the urubu watches us—you must return to the zoo of intellects
the urubu takes root in the orange ulcer sky
where are you going
juggler windmill hairstyles all the sea-eagles
are cankered
egg-nog

from Circus

3

this is only the beginning
my soul a paper flower workshop again
I haven't forgotten my mother however
the last agreement (so favourable)
she would forgive me I think
it's late
you find discordant drum-beats in every corner
if only I could sing
always the same always somewhere
this dazzling light the ants the transparency
bursting out of my guilty hand
I'll leave
the carved wooden madonna is the poster the censure
opaque silence broken by the irregular tick
it's my heart which prolongs the 5th measure
and glory
glimpsed
the velvet curtain after the final march
with the most subtle modulation do you also think of me
four figures on the wall
with the last worry
why search
and there's a ringing which will never end

6

—who knows the measured and exact force of blows
neither too weak nor too strong
my legs are long and slender
flowed from a crevasse of the steel sun
we are honest men
organization of the importance of fat bouncing lamps
let's dance let's shout
I love you the train leaves each day
let's drink electric arc

the whore's song
the dangerous operation

hand-pink tree flower
soothes my tears
offer sisterly souls
to things

splendour and subtlety
have gnawed my heart
I turn endlessly
my arms spiral to the sky

it's cold
listen mother
and think of me
now

the last arrived from the tropics
equinox flower white-tailed phaeton
driving towards amsterdam around a table and the valve
of the second fog

total circuit by the moon and colour

the iron eye will change to gold
the compasses have put flowers in our ear-drums
watch for the fabulous prayer sir
tropical
on the eiffel tower's violin and star chimes
the olives swell pac pac and will symmetrically crystalize
everywhere
lemon
the ten sou piece
sundays have brilliantly fondled god dada dance
sharing the cereals
the rain
newspaper
slowly slowly
butterflies five yards long disintegrate like mirrors
like the flight of night rivers climbs with the fire
towards the milky way
the ways of light the hair of irregular rains
and the artificial summer-houses that fly age in your heart
when you think I see
morning
that screams
the cells dilate
bridges stretch and rise up in the air to scream
around magnetic poles the rays arrange themselves like
peacocks' feathers
boreal
and the waterfalls do you see? arrange themselves in their own light
at the north pole a huge peacock will slowly unfurl the sun
at the other pole will be the night of serpent-eating colours
slide yellow
the bells

nervous
to clear it up the reds will march
when 1 ask how
the deeps shout
lord my geometry

the death of guillaume apollinaire

we know nothing
we knew nothing of grief
the bitter season of cold
carves long scars in our muscles
he would have sooner loved the joy of victory
wise with quiet sadnesses   caged
can do nothing
if snow fell upwards
if the sun rose here during the night
to warm us
and the trees hung with their wreath
—the only tear—
if the birds were among us to be reflected
in the quiet lake above our heads
ONE WOULD UNDERSTAND
death would be a fine long journey
and limitless holidays for flesh structures and bones

from cinema calendar of the abstract heart

9

the fibres give in to your starry warmth
a lamp is called green and sees
carefully stepping into a season of fever
the wind has swept the rivers' magic
and I've perforated the nerve
by the clear frozen lake
has snapped the sabre
but the dance of round terrace tables
shuts in the shock of the marble shudder
new sober

15

on the white threads of withered midnight
meet waterproof lunatic messenger
bulb rubber woman of greenery in
kilometres
the subterranean mesh of the touch

18

purgatory announces the grand festival
the love policeman who pisses so quickly
cock and ice go to bed under an amorous gaze
large lamp stomachs virgin mary
rue st-jacques the pretty boys set off
towards the bells of the white aorta dawn
the devil's water weeps on my reason

maison flac

bugles let out the great and glassy news animals of the maritime service
air balloon forester all that exists rides from brightness the life
the angel has white haunches waterproof virility
snow licks the road and the lily verifies the virgin
$^3/_{25}$ of altitude a new meridian passes by here
extended arc of my heart typewriter for the stars
which told you 'chopped foam of great sadness-clocks'
told you a word you can't find in Larousse
and wants to reach your height

what smoke from a lightning-tube forces
ours against the eternal and multiform sail
here men are not assassinated on the terraces
which colour with a close succession of slow ways

we try unheard of things
illusions small written quartos of chromatic souls and pictures
we carry all the tinkling uproar that we cause
for the major festivals on the viaducts and for the animals

the figure of an eight part dance on meteor and violin
the game of glasses the year which passes
let's drink a cup I'm the mad friah
sky ink mead lake
hazy wine plop in the hammock

say the offertory tranquil and peaceful
he scrapes the sky with his nails
and the sky-scraper is only his shadow
in a dressing gown

the year will pass among the palm and banana trees burst out with
    a halo in ice cubes
simple productive vast music surging safely
and the crimson bread in the future and fruitful season
old engravings prettily coloured of kings hunting

pipe and matches in the vase under the ace of spades piper with
the birds and cool skies a boat ready at the point
the motor rock in the sparkling of good news the eiffel tower plays
    a rebeck
here each chair is soft and comfortable as an archbishop
ascetic ventures monks guaranteed at all prices—
                    here ladies—Maison Flac

railway station

dance shout smash
travel I wait on the bench
all the same what? my nerves are hushes
of interrupted moments

read peacefully
turnings-round
the newspaper
watch who goes by

I don't know
if I'm all alone
the light listens but on what
side and why

the flight of a burning bird
is my male strength under the dome
I seek refuge in the fiery depth
stealing the ruby

I've given my soul
to the white stone
precise and wise
unadvertised god

order in friendship
say: the fire's grief
has blackened my eyes
and I've thrown them into the waterfall

leave
see my face
in the evening's circle or in the suitcase
or in the snow cage

I leave this evening
the spark weeps
in my bed in the factory
dogs and jaguars howl

have you too given your soul
to the wrist-stone
oblong skulled juggler
my brother climbs

I was honest
sister infinite
finished for this
night

hearts of pharmacies plants
open in the gentle light of the spheres
and religion's liquors it's true
lions and clowns

the white leprous giant in the countryside

the salt collects in a constellation of birds on the padded tumour
in his lungs the starfish and bugs sway
the microbes crystallize into palms of swaying muscles
good morning without a cigarette tzantzantza ganga
boozdooc zdooc nfoonfa mbaah nfoonfa
macrocystic perifera to embrace the boats surgeon of boats moist
        clean scar
languor of flashing lights
the boats nfoonfa nfoonfa nfoonfa
I stick candles in his ears ganganfah helican and boxer on the hotel
   violin balcony in baobabs of flames
the flames spread out like a growth of sponges

the flames are sponges nganga and strike
the ladders rise like the blood ganga
the ferns towards the wool steppes my fortune towards the waterfalls
the flames glass sponges the palliasses wounds palliasses
the palliasses fall wancanca aha bzdooc the butterflies
the scissors the scissors the scissors and the shadows
the scissors and the clouds the scissors the ships
the thermometer watches the ultra-red gmbababa
bertha my education my tail is cold and monochrome nfooa looa la
the orange mushrooms and the family of sounds further to starboard
at the beginning at the beginning the triangle and the travellers'
      tree at the beginning
my brains set out towards the hyperbole
caolin swarms in his skull-box
dalibooli obak and tombo and tombo his belly's a bass drum
here the drum-major and castanets step in
for there are zigzags on his soul and lots of rrrrrrrrrrrrrr here the
      reader starts to scream

he starts to scream starts to scream then in his scream there are
      flutes which multiply corals
the reader wants to die perhaps or dance and starts to scream
he's skinny stupid dirty he doesn't understand my verses he
      screams
he's cock-eyed
there are zigzags on his soul and lots of rrrrrrr
nbaze baze baze look at the undersea tiara which comes undone in
      golden seaweed
hozondrac trac
nfoonda nbababa nfoonda tata
nbababa

the great lament over my obscurity

1

cold whirlwind bloody zigzag
I'm soulless friendless brainless waterfall lord
I don't get letters regularly from my mother
that must come through russia norway or england
red-spiralled memories burn my brain on the steps of the amphitheatre
and like a flashing-sign for my soul the sphere's flashing misfortune
light tower the fertile wheel of blue ants
halo acute drought of sorrows

come near me don't let the prayer trouble you it goes down into
        the earth like the diving-suits that'll be invented
then the iron obscurity will change into wine and salt
simplicity our plants' lightning-rod beware
the lightning-rods that gather like spiders
thus I become the crown of a gigantic christ
shapeless country voltaic arc

the snow eagles will come and feed the rock
where the deep clay will change into milk
and the milk will disturb the night chains rattle
the rain will forge heavy
chains
will shape spokes in the space of the wheels
the sceptre in the middle among the branches
the old newspapers tapestries
a paralytic
halo drought
fertile wheel of blue ants
lord goldfinger sphinx cooker
why do I strangle it why
after the thunderbolt the route-march will shatter
my despair tin iron pipe but why why then?

◄

always this way this way but the road
you mut be my rain my circuit my pharmacy naked May raingel
    naked May raingel do you want

2

watch my hair's grown
my brain's springs are yellowed lizards that
liquefy
sometimes
the holed
hanged man
tree
the soldier
in muddy regions where birds are glued together in silence
star knight
faded tapestries
acid that doesn't burn like the caged panthers
the water jet escapes and rises
towards the other colours

tremors
suffering my daughter of the blue and distant nothing
my head is empty as a hotel closet
tell me slowly the poor's fishes tremble and break
when do you want to leave
the sand
passport
desire
the bridge breaking with the third opposition
the space
police
the heavy
emperor
sand
what a piece of furniture what a lamp to invent for your soul
paper gas september

in the printing-press
I love you the lemons that swell on ice separate us my mother my
          veins along the lord
my mother
my mother my mother you wait in the snow-drift electricity
fabulous
discipline
the leaves arrange themselves in wing formations calm us on an
          island and ascend like the order of archangels
white fire

3

at our house the clock flowers light up and feathers surround the light
the distant sulphur morning cows lick salt lilies
my son
my son

let's always drag by the colour of the world
that looks bluer than the metro and astronomy
we're too thin
we've no mouths
our legs are stiff and knock together
our faces aren't star-like
crystal points on many a fire the mad basilica
burnt: zigzags crack
telephone
to bite the bonds turn to liquid
the arc
to climb
the starry
memory
to the north by its double fruit
like raw flesh
famine fire blood

drugstore-conscience

the lamp of a lily will bear so great a prince
that the water-jets will expand the factories
and the leech changing into a sickness tree
I'm looking for the root unshakable lord unshakable lord
why then yes you'll learn
come spiralling towards the useless tear

humid parrot
lignite cactus swell up between the black cow's horns
the parrot hollows out the tower the holy mannequin

in your heart there's a child—a lamp
the doctor declares he won't last the night

then he leaves in short sharp lines silence siliceous formation

when the hunted wolf rests on the white
the chosen one hunts his inmates
displaying flora descended from death which will be the reason
and the cardinal of france will appear
the three lilies stunning clarity electric virtue
long dry red painting fishes and letters under the colour

the leper giant of the countryside
comes to a standstill between two towns
he has streams cadence and the hills' tortoises slowly assemble
he spits out sand kneads his wool lungs for them to grow clearer
the soul and nightingale whirl round in his laughter—sunflower
he wants to pluck the rainbow my heart is a paper starfish

in missouri in brazil in the west indies
if you think if you're happy reader you become transparent for a moment
your transparent sponge brain
and in this transparency there'll be another more distant transparency
distant when a new animal will turn blue in this transparency

small town in Siberia

a blue light that holds us flattened on the ceiling
it's as always my friend like a label of hell's gates stuck on a
          medicine bottle
it's the quiet house my friend shudders
and then the heavy bowed dance
presents old age skipping hour by hour on the clock face
the unsullied necklace of cut loco lamps comes down among us
          now and then
and collapses you call that silence to drink tin roofs herring tin's
          gleam and my seemly heart on some low houses lower higher
          lower on which I want to run and rub my hands against the hard
          bread-crumb covered table sleep oh yes if only one could
the train once more the fool spectacle of the dandy's tower I'm
          left on the bench
what does the fool the dandy the newspaper what's going to
          happen matter it's cold I'm waiting speak up
hearts and eyes roll in my mouth
get moving
and little children in the blood
(is it the angel? I'm talking about the one who's approaching)
let's run even faster
always everywhere we'll be left surrounded by darkened windows

instant our brother

nothing goes up nothing comes down no sideways movement
he gets up
nothing stirs neither being or non-being or idea or the shackled
       prisoner or the tramway
he hears nothing but himself
understands nothing but the chairs the stone the cold the water—
knows passes through the solid matter
not needing his eyes any more he throws them into the street
last gleam of blood in the darkness
last greeting
he tears out his tongue—flame transfixed by a star
soothed
autumn dead like a red palm leaf

and reabsorbs what he denied and dissolved projects it into the
       other hemisphere second season of existence as nails and hairs
       grow and come back

glass to pass through peaceful

the joy of lines wind around you soul's central heating
smoke speed steel smoke
geography of silk embroideries
colonised with flowering sponges
the song crystallized
in the
body's vase with the smoke flower

the black's vibration
in your blood
in your blood of the evening's intelligence and wisdom
a blue wrinkled eye in a clear glass
I love you I love you
a vertical comes down into my tiredness which no longer enlightens me
my heart muffled in an old newspaper
you can bite it: whistle
let's go

the clouds set in ranks in the officers' fever
the bridges mangle your poor body is very large these milky way
        scissors and cut out the memory in green shapes
in one direction always in the same direction
expanding always expanding

retreat

birds childhood ploughs quick
inns
battle at the pyramids
18th brumaire
the cat the cat is saved
entrance
cry
valmy
long live turn red
cry
in the hole trumpet small slow bells
cry
the chapped hands of trees order
cry
to him
post
to the white to the bird
let's cry
you cry
slide

you wear nailed on your scars moon proverbs
tanned moon spread your diaphragm on the horizon
moon eye tanned in a black viscous liquid
vibrations the deafman
heavy animals fleeing in tangent circles
of muscles tar heat
the pipes bend braid
the bowels
blue

springtime

with your beautiful fingernails
put the child in the vase in the middle of the night
and the sore
a rose of winds
the thunder in feathers see
an evil water flows with the limbs of the antelope

suffer below have you found cows birds?
the thirst the venom of the peacock in the cage
the king in exile through the clearness of the pit slowly mummifies
in the vegetable garden
sow crushed locusts
plant ants' hearts in the salt fog a lamp drags its tail over the sky
the tiny glitter of glass objects in the bellies of fleeing deer
on the tips of short black branches for a cry

notes

strange double-masked woman
white sweep of an obscene dance
come close to me only chord
of weary limbs
opinions of no special importance
suspicious blue ebony blood
and the tip

hide your longing
behind the eight-twenty death
if I could start the night again this morning
dieci soldi: there
my soul

you won't have this evening
the last refinement of my virility
for a long time I've gone beyond the illusory industry
where at this moment you drag out your sun rotten existence

so I pass you pass like the mother the child
slowly more quickly slowly
one after the other or all together
golden pimp's eye of timid eternity
vanishes
bell of a cheap idea
midwife queen
and it's all quite devoid of interest

dada song

1

the song of a dadaist
who had dada in his heart
so over-taxed his ticker
that had dada in its heart

the elevator carried a king
weighty brittle independent
he cut off his long right arm
sent it to the pope in rome

that's why
the elevator
no longer had dada in its heart

eat chocolate
wash your brain
dada
dada
drink water

2

the song of a dadaist
who wasn't glad wasn't sad
and was in love with a lady cyclist
who wasn't glad wasn't sad

but the husband on new year's day
knew all and in a fit
dispatched to the vatican
their two bodies in three suitcases

neither the lover
nor the lady cyclist
were glad or sad any longer

eat excellent brains
wash your soldier
dada
dada
drink water

3

the song of a cyclist
who was dada-hearted
who was then a dadaist
like all the dada-hearted

a snake was wearing gloves
he quickly shut the valve
popped on some snake skin gloves
and came and kissed the pope

it's touching
belly in flower
no longer had dada in its heart

drink bird milk
wash your chocolates
dada
dada
eat veal

on a sun-ripple

mornings drown the desires muscles and fruits
in the raw and secret liquor
soot woven in golden ingots
covers the night clawed by brief patterns

on a new made horizon
a water drapery running vast alive
grates small special coefficient
of my love
in the suddenly opened door

harassed by eclipsed desires
tearful hurried trembling
you shed your leaves in the hope of secret harmony
the fickleness of the water slides on your body with the sun

through the parted miracle you catch a glimpse of the mask
never clear never new
you go on it's life that makes the crank-arm work
and that's why the eyes roll in their why

the advantage of blood through the cry of the mist
a fan of flames on the volcano you know
that the moods of the grave
have accompanied all songs of ardour
to that glimpse
the world
a hat with flowers
the world
a violin playing a flower
the world
a ring made for a flower

a flower flower for the bouquet of flowers flowers
a cigarette-holder filled with flowers
a small loco with eyes of flowers
a pair of gloves for flowers
made of flowers like flowers flowers flowers of flowers
and an egg

vegetable swallow

two smiles meet towards
the child—a wheel of my zeal
the bloody baggage of creatures
made flesh in physical legends—lives

the nimble stags storms cloud over
rain falls under the scissors of
the dark hairdresser—furiously
swimming under the clashing arpeggios

in the machine's sap grass
grows around with sharp eyes
here the share of our caresses
dead and departed with the waves

gives itself up to the judgement of time
parted by the meridian of hairs
noon strikes in our hands
the spices of human pleasures

around

1

the terrace is full
of salty murmurs
the dress and even
the pleats of the sun

lost today
almost accessible
to the vertigo dullness
ended at midnight

the sophisticated animal
with his illusions
opens up the flight
from educational clarity

and the withered victim
expertly hunted
bright red icicles
thick mocking

the crazy lover
hungry for the dark
a necklace of moods
gentle and savage

heavy with sun
like a fiesta
catches the eye
at the window

glides on sandals
from sun soundings
to the picture puzzle of the seas
advertisements for evil

the curly flowers
on holiday
hats in a burst
of vegetable elegance

on the rocks the lemons
porous solemn
the hotel charges
are increased with the landscape

the natty tie
tied in an alibi
of disconcerting nights
wasted in talk

vices perfumes
the quick excuses
of houses flowers
and wines peace

the deathly sound
and immoralities
sweet breeze bandage
they pass with age

dreadful diseases
measured my dear
to the degree of alcohol
under the branches of journeys

imperceptibly clear
the keys to the bonds
didn't you know
were our medicines

the grave women
at the end of cruel hands
towns of weariness
dried like figs

put it all in the cupboard
of smoked memories
goodbye goodbye
my dear these earthly games

2

when the fish rows
the talk of the lake
when it plays the scale
the strolling women

when the spinster bird
swallows her life
with pretty songs
lights the air chain

I think of your extravagance
woken in scarfs of hurricane
which creases the curls of the mountains
separates the bright from the dull pleasure

the greetings of your lips
disturb me may the rain
empty the river
that my sky drinks

I confide in murmurs
of the seated hours
why should I be sorry
sorry sorry

but the forest down there
only a few yards away
simmers with violence
in the shop of horizons

though the delicate lashes
have caught in their adornments
the insect of your slow breath
I eternally long for it

the lace sweet lady
is ashes to the cloud
without the wheel of wise thoughts
I don't venture on the roads

the roads are bad
for there's no more money in the coffers
exports are like caresses
they don't pay taxes at the customs

lady lady if you knew
how much I love you and idolize you
you wouldn't leave without an insurance
on the life I have in mind

but it's not retrospective
the story of the morning fate
now it's late late
in the shoe of the ravine

and what are you doing about the prescriptions
of the doctor bursting out of the fine
knowledge with his ripe and handsome temples?
I pack my things she replied

so january crumbles
february march april may
june february march and the
years of counted feathers—but

by the length of virile cheers from the lamps
the bandits knew of her wealth
and neatly cut up
her fine body of charming flesh

oh the beasts the filth
but I'd rather keep quiet
the solitary scorching regret
suits me much better

and I value my beauty
my health my gaiety
my liberty my equality
my fraternity and what I've got to say

3

the call of his fine heart
grand like a gentleman
begins here in his castle
in the midst of hearts

under the clothing of stones
the padlock lays itself open to the mysteries
let them fall on their gums
the sensual gods of late hours

the sharp strength of the bells
stops the gossiping
the magic cows are locked up
in the black heart of the garage

soon no doubt
the slanting darkness
ancient with gulls
nailed and hairy

she-wolf of lilacs
slow like the regular
twitch of sleepers
the tactful remorse

of lovers and springs
and sleep lays waste
air and feathers
with the thrashing wheels of steamships

when quick motherly
doubt provokes us
and threatens us I leave
my body adrift

always weary fragile
touched up with paint
the thoughtless laughter
and embellished by all that

the breast of the façade
improved by a tenor
it was a lost wave
in the slide of the golden sea

smoothing out the cable the captain
dreams of happiness cleaned
like a revolver—come
I'll put my omissions on your wound

far from the famous wreck
of the storm of abandoned orangeade
I'll put my bears in a cage
and my hard feelings to the test

of desire on the other shore
of your arms with their enclosed rays
the sad metal of the water
at the flute-like base of your brain

I'll never never dare
to give you my voice frozen
the live metal of the water
at the flute-like base of your brain

where for a long time scepticism
I considered the civil avalanche
the solemn metal of the water
at the flute-like base of your ear

may winter come as a friend
held up in its lottery
may the sack of snow be shaken
in the transformations of gold bearing gods

may the motions of things be scattered
and the clarinet of the buskin be pulled off
may people look at me sideways
when put out by the nocturnal cold

may the music be frozen on the gospel
and may we burst in clever dreams
with a strong voice the reflections
will leave the house but it isn't my fault

but what use since I love you
to conquer the cries of the world

the condemned

to better conceal his human wreck
from the busy eyes of traders
in souls and innumerable wrongs in Ithaca
he destroys his travelling kit

when one talks to him of the oiled skins of athletes
the flocks of sheep in shorthand symbols
that his mistress draws in the air with her lashes
his life is chained to the ringing links of holiday

the night is bitter
I know why
it's when the wolf
rubs himself against the stone

there the earth is grinding
and putting the whip-like tracks in order
no chasm's sneers have ever been more trampled
by heavy breasts burst forth on the threshold of your mouth

the arms of planets and flowering torments at the end
by the charred fingers of calls greetings and roots
make the expected irruption through the flames
along fissures that I can only measure by your laughter

by the immeasurable breath that has fled the sun of your laughter

from Mr AA the antiphilosopher

1

Captain!
the thunderbolts, the full might of the waterfall menaces us, the knot of serpents, the cat-o'-nine-tails, triumphantly march into countries contaminated with continual strife;

Captain!

all the accusations of ill-treated animals, yawn, in bites above the bed, in rose-windows of blood, the rain of stone teeth and the excrement stains in the cages shroud us in endless snowlike cloaks;

Captain!

the brightness of the coal becoming seal, lightning, insect under your eyes, the squadrons of moonstruck people, the monsters on wheels, the screams of mechanical sleepwalkers, the liquid stomachs on silver salvers, the cruelties of carnivorous flowers will overrun the simple country day and the cinema of your sleep;

Captain!

beware of blue eyes.

23

the dwarf in his cornet

Who's calling me in the hole upholstered with bits of fluff, it's me replied the open earth, the couches hardened with unbreakable patience, the floor's jaw.

The hand that the cloud offers us touches the eye with my very best wishes. Who's calling me it's you yes it's me it's you yes it's you.

Does he think then I am the millimetre does he think why am I not the traveller of phrase tubes does he think why I am not the locomotive's eye on paper holiday does he think why am I not the arab horse's millimetre and some lumps of coal I swing symmetry and with my wing touch the sound of the pagoda's walls.

At these words, the English woman began to scream: rape rape. The tree was travelling incognito. He came to table looking very embarrassed. The English woman was finishing her day with irritated swoons, indignant flutes, ultimatums to life, voice vivisections. No one frowned on her pleasure. The other one, the one that I said in the previous chapter had an umbrella instead of a head and in his build resembled an armchair (a real man, no matter what you put inside), was singing:

landscapes and accidents

neat avenues polished
the dawn cafe where the summer proverb will come out
given for the benefit of all travelling plans
strung along the arcades of flutes
the wax navel melts
all the little puppets thus on the end truck
where are we going asks the gentleman who's had disappointments
now there's the laughter that trickles
these are slices of glass breasts
it's a love-meter
it's the perfected threat of a bell umbrella beating
and the passport for the upper-story of the cupboard opens
there's a free glacier and the birds
we notice there the microphone
amplifying the steps and words that daren't sound any more
stay as it were in their shells
but you see them as these are eyes
that's where an hour of oblivion leads
the ruby bracelet grows on your cheek
with flame acid drops
the foliage of veins spreads with the slowness of thirst
it's a real disaster
that the throbbings of walls of houses explains and accompanies
a car
a young girl lies stretched out on the pavement
a damp handkerchief
an accident like any other you'll say
there's where an hour of oblivion leads
nobody asks for your participation
in the excited speculation around a handkerchief of crushed oblivion
the social need does not justify it
however there's where an hour of oblivion leads

with unanimous abstentions when a foreseen collision is the matter
between the bones and the numerous injured at large
locomotive grief that quickly goes in all directions
the seismographs sound the earth
money transactions
the panic the ties are tied and untied by numbers
but the machine will never
record the congestion of a nerve-wracked hour
this fine and flowing writing of the body
shows the rivers on its map

there's where an hour of oblivion leads
how do you expect to understand what no one else has yet understood
I scratch the organs one after the other
an elegant dance for loneliness when language is stuck to the palate
an icy museum postage-stamp on the horror of permanently blank
          window-panes

each one of us has a reservoir of events
that will happen in the most convenient order of exit
they'll come out like parrots and their phrases
without worrying themselves about the accuracy of their interesting
observations
there's where an hour of oblivion leads
in the smoke-blackened oat tunnels

Way

what is this road that separates us
across which I hold out the hand of my thoughts
a flower is written at the end of each finger
and the end of the road is a flower which walks with you

Approach

magic step of unfinished nights
nights gulped down in haste bitter drinks gulped down in haste
nights buried under the muddy mat of our slow passions
barren dreams in far looks of pecking crows

soiled sodden night rags we have built
within us each one of us a coloured tower so lofty
that the view is no longer blocked beyond mountains and waters
that the sky no longer turns away from our star nets
that the clouds lie down at our feet like hunting dogs
and we can stare into the sun until oblivion

and yet my peace only finds its reason
in the nest of your arms the night tide
after the burst of squalling storms streams down death
it's the loose body of an earthly suit of armour
that drops away from the necklace of our dreams of oblivion

Volt

the leaning towers the slanted skies
cars falling into the void of roads
animals lining the country roads
with branches covered in liberal properties
and leaf-like birds on their heads
you walk but it's another who follows in your footsteps
distilling her spite through scraps of memory and arithmetic
wrapped in a gown the curdled sound of capitals nearly muffled

the seething town thick with proud calls and lights
boils over with the stewpan of its eyelids
its tears flow in streams of low populations
on the sterile plain towards the flesh and lava smoothes
shadowy mountains the apocalyptic temptations

lost in the geography of a memory and a dark rose
I prowl the narrow streets around you
while you too you prowl other greater streets
around something

Rule

the clashing seas spread the ocean of their idleness
in the beds with white foam sheets
at the sound of pages of waves turned by the reader of
the unsated sky
the loving and steady caress of clouds
dissolves behind the mist
the long awaited promise on the horizon of your smile

the land at its bursting point reveals the young white stone
of a giant's firm breast offered for the length of time
and the wind bites its lips in its black rage

smashed is the clarity passing through the glasses of our lives
the wind chokes the word in the village's throat poor village
its life of strange revelations

shattered is the chain of words covered in winters and dramas
which connected the intimate revelations of our lives

and the wind spits in our face
the untiring brutality of it all

Palm Grove

what will you think in the evening when stretched out on the shore
the untiring purring that an ultimate fate grinds
between the stones of its lock amid the dry leaf
right next to your ears will bring forth from this world
and the smooth pallor and the barren memory

what will you do in the evening that hung on a thought
pursuing words the occult games
or their subtle flights under the slag-heaps
for you alone unseen the signal will come
to force your way among the light ways

it will tell you in the evening that listening at the door
impatient at all the inexhaustible fears
the blindman who knocks at the door
brings blindness to all those who see him
and touch the ringing forehead on the door step

who will tell you in the evening that it was in the evening the blindman
the hard dull breast crossed
with fruitless sowings with crying
waters of everlasting echoes heavy
like the fearful and wan seas

it was one evening carved by the throbbing waters
that your eyes invented and gave as your share to love
and the quick gasps spanned the hill
where its mourning was held ready to attack
the stammering reason to secretly hate

it was the evening when the old truth
was ringing below in small old wooden bells

of harmless truths were rubbing the cattle below
against the lotus fibre and the cliff eyes
were walking on words so mild was the evening below

it was that evening that the earth stuffed with zebus
hardened by the blows of so many insatiable middays
and shadow-flecked mangroves—so that its light started
such a jackal's howl—crushed the column
of sleeping mountains in the gaunt sand

the feeble leap of silence in the rough drafts of the wait
and after the wait silence again and the void
it was no longer the evening of smoking rays
nor the timid mouth seeking to know
the fiddle the squill and in the bush the lavender eyebrows

it was no longer the gay tambourine of pebbles and tridactyls
the languid evening unfurling with its silky glow
the salt marshes and the night silt covered in owls
have swooped down on us blazing saxifrages
cedars corianders maples

it was no longer the evening stretched out on the shore's carpet
        which wears away
from now on the ocean thick with living loopholes hugs the horizon
ocean boiling in the upturned mountains
a posthumous people climbs up your foam peaks
where the sun casts the shadow eternally bound to our hours' narrowness

blind patience blind bundle of rags
pulled by the string that a flashing eye guides
along the road that the deceitful starfish have stolen from the stars
in the hollow of our visits we only know of the dreams
the ample harvest of the luminous never

and when the lithophonic heart takes hold of the spirals
where the elliptical laburnum veins open
our brains clumsily move off and walk
walk until the rough convulsion of the night's asphalt
clumsily tossed about on the night's rump

and overcome by so much spacious rest
all the landscape's family walks rustling at our side
and the night walks furtively with the step of the conquered
up to the river where death soaks itself
a slow pause for clarity in the confusion of whistles

the tangle of serpents the land of stones and tears
and under each stone the warmth of a tear
right next to a flash's atom and broodily gazing at fate
which will tell us one day cheek to cheek the magic tenderness
that plays tricks on the setting sun

and the steel hand at the neck of the bleeding staircase
laughs at never passing through the door when leaving
an insect juggler of refined ancient cruelties
a threat at least an earnestness
laughs at never passing through the door when entering

it's night friends overcast night
which laughs at never passing through the door singing
and the house is pregnant with it
another revenge the slowest
grief-stricken till no longer knowing it

from The Approximate Man

13 (an extract)

who will free us from the encumbrance of possessions and flesh
the applause of the sea breaks over you
the tragic and taut sea wall on the first step of the amphitheatre
old stone wrinkle on the worn forehead of the world
the wreckage and rubbish thrown into the sea
and the sea's into the world
the careworn wrinkle of earth crowded
tied down in the deep of sea shadows
cramped in the darkness of the stern fearless of the future
meeting with claws striding erect in the waves
wrinkle sodden with the inconceivable curse of time
until the end of time
until the exhaustion of cyclones in their elysian storerooms
sad little life beaten at every step
tumbled knocked hurried sad life
sad life harassed by the wild omens trampled on
and yet: the jaws of immovable eternity and insolence
fortified and crenellated right up to the apex of god
that no eye has been able to reach
no joy able to warm with human tenderness
but what use to climb the magpie to filter the clouds
when human kindness no longer knows how to warm my joys
what does a friend matter alone at night boredom
I'm all soft bread inside death friend
and the degree of cold increases in me each day friend
becomes friend what does the custom matter
what does a friend matter alone at night boredom
one day one day one day I'll put on the cloak of eternal warmth
buried forgotten by others in their turn forgotten by others
if I could only gain the glowing forgotten

from budding traps

10

in the footsteps that it contrives
the shaggy hill attaches itself to the dark
pain thirst where there's no more room
and can't find itself among the other tracks

no longer knows how to rest in the well of incantations
an anguish breaks the leaf
that on the rare halts a night for the blind
unearths fear

and from the sunny side invisible on my side
another shiver walks over the stones of eyes
with your hands full of blessings
full of worlds that rise in me

bound in the irons of remembrance
in a strangled voice
from one night to the other
without laughing at a life where the impossible fades away

from where the wolves drink

13

when leaves press against leaves and mate their lithe wet bodies
and cover themselves in the sensations of the first dew
in the heart of a song
withered with lips around the bed
there are eyes that can't fall asleep
jealously cut down to the level of baby words
to revive night rags
to make the hot dust of our hands swirl round wildly
in the hermit's cramp
when fear lies down in the fresh grave
of our body with the living signs of fire
of earth robbed at ancient doors
pausing mixed with grass ash which no longer knows how to grow
or hang its head in the rent of an undergrowth kiss

in the breast of the sun the ants
and not a grain of sand passes through the head's sieve
a cement of old gold and summer
on the bird's hurried steps
where the fearful gulp starts along the new skin
of an amorous and lost road slowly with fruits

the retreat of lonely blood
and the lake of blood in a desert where wings
transparent during calms
gather into grass of silence
as soft as full
as breasts in tears bathed in caresses
and suddenly the gaping wound
of so much life glowing with the colour's cries
and cracking
and of depression

from the well-digger of looks

5

alone in an ample soul I've seen so many chances lost
in the futile scale of light
that proud as solitude has engulfed the abyss in the
universal colour which leads me

it's a real alcohol in your eyes
a rough swarming of planets
and the anchor hugged to your breast
where winds beat together
wasn't this the radiant fruit on the cotton barn's floor
roads dammed by the sea's teeth
and your hair in the wind that weeps
a new star would register on the hand's flora
a life made of deep silence strength
to the limits of the storm

the contemplation of pools of banners where dead towns of waves mingle
without the noise of windows on the sky of sharks
flee neglects of memory
where dull ways crawl
towards some dead-end tolling with bells
where the thread of light is caught
in its soft significance of power and right

is it kind the unknown roofs
which the snow of continual failures of actions
penetrates darker than ever
where we dream the same shore
and on the fallow skeleton
the unpunished blossoms go adrift

7

on the horizon the orisons of life always soar
in disorder
the cork is a deer the deer is a leaf
a bejewelled morning a dress of fluttering hands
that flee the earth

a face that hurries in the night
the anxieties on the shore
a light that wanders without knowing itself
a woman who reluctantly inhabits it
the snow covers it on the forbidden summits
a single shadow finds it
a single one that searches for it that doesn't question
the birth of shadows

8

strange unexpected news knocked at the door
in the mouth of the street the acrobat was playing dice
come in he said and the light went on
knock he said at the door further along
the far far waters
higher than the birth of waters
and the dead women follow us right up to each doorstep
come in he said and the light went on
no one had knocked
again it was the loneliness the flash of lightning that melts inside
and nothing exhausted the vast expanse of the outline of shores

I've rediscovered them buried voiceless
solitary at the bottom of their looks of delicate cracks
in the cold shaft a single word is to say
that doesn't find the power of the game

the rivers follow me where I no longer hold myself responsible
my steps are intercepted the answers expected
there are no more caresses in the look of eyes
except in your eyes where bodies bleed
woman whose looks are locked in the looks of others
and the streets pass like queens where the women always new
in the light of the nest are counted

from night summary

5

sighs become fur hours the quick voice
and I've lived remorselessly like a song in their water
impassive a new tenderness unrolls at the silk auction
what happened to the love then before your lavender eyes
cables cut down to the level of sand feet
the whistle come from the long wide spaces of flat prayers
of the return that shows the moist soft fairy happenings
this black night that shines with such lasting delight that the light
        on bulls' horns flounders
oh bottle of chattering seas—what happened to love then—
refloating the greys cheering the chimney fires
like a great simplicity in love
like no one knew how to keep it out of the way of demented leaves
suffocated walls fixed eyes or the card-sharp who even plays with
        life in the wards' game
and out of despair at the noises of schoolchildren
a calm and unfaltering song composes
words that snap in the wind of barges under oak boots
what happened to love then and my voice falls silent
as a sledge-hammer rebounds into the void
a calm song not another rent
a clock missing
a fox down-stream
a doll missing
another in the distance
who am I what am I fleeing
at the door of azaleas another door

on the road of sea stars

to Federico Garcia Lorca

what wind blows on the world's loneliness
that I remember dear ones
frail griefs breathed by death
above time's clumsy hunts
the storm rejoiced its end nearer
that the sand had yet to round its hard haunch
but on the mountains pockets of fire
put out without fail their prey's light
wan and short such a friend dies
whose outline nobody can describe anymore with words
and no call on the horizon has time to help
a description only measurable until his disappearance

and so from one flash to the other
the animal always offers its sharp rump
through the hostile centuries
across fields some for pageants others for greed
and in its breaking is outlined the memory
like the wood which creaks as a sign of presence
and jarring necessity

there are also the fruits
and I don't forget the wheat
and the sweat which made it grow rises in your throat
we know however the price of grief
the wings of oblivion and the endless drillings
on the surface of life
words that can't grasp facts
barely usable for laughter

the horse of the night has galloped from the trees to the sea
and joined the reins of a thousand kindly shadows
he's dragged along hedgerows
where men's breasts hold back the onslaught
with all the murmurings caught in his flanks
among the immense roarings that catch up with themselves
while fleeing the force of immeasurable waters
they followed one another while minute murmurs
weren't engulfed and survived
in unconquerable loneliness where passed tunnels
forests flocks of towns harnessed seas
a lone man with the breath of several countries
joined in the waterfall and sliding on a smooth wave
of unknown fire that sometimes gets into the night
to the loss of those who are joined in sleep
in their deep memory

but let's talk no more of those who are bound
to the fragile branches to the evil moods of nature
even those that suffer the rough blows
offer their necks and the stiff boots of conquerors
thud on the carpet of their bodies
when the birds don't peck the sun seeds
they've left no memory
the birds look for other spring jobs
in the selfish hope of sinecures
in charming flocks of bewilderments
the wind on their heels
may the desert spare them

to hell with the subtle warnings
the pastimes poppies & Co.
the cold gnaws
fear mounts
the tree dries up
the man splits

shutters bang
fear mounts
no word is kind enough
to bring back the child of the roads
who gets lost in the head
of a man on the season's edge
he watches the heavens
and watches the abyss
water-tight compartments
smoke in the gorge
the roof crumbles away
but the famous animal buttressed
in the tension of muscles and twisted in the spasm
of the vertical flight from the flash from rock to rock
breaks loose longing for joy
the morning remakes its world
according to its yoke

sea-robber
you stoop under the hope
and rise and each time you bow to the drunken sea at your feet
on the road of sea stars
led on by columns of uncertainty
you stoop you rise
greetings stirred by bands
and on the pile you must go on however
even in avoiding the beauties you must go on however
you stoop
on the road of sea stars
my brothers howl with grief at the other end
they must be taken whole
these are the hands of the sea
that are offered to nobodies
glorious road on the road of sea stars
'alcachofas[†] alcachofas' it's my fine Madrid

[†] *alcachofas* (Spanish)—artichokes

with its tin eyes and fruity voice
which is open to all the winds
waves of iron waves of fire
I mean sea splendours
they must be taken whole
those in the knocked-down broken branches
on the road of sea stars
where does this road lead it leads to grief
men fall when they want to stand erect
men sing as they've tasted death
however you must go on
go on over
the road of sea stars through columns of uncertainty
but you get tangled in the liana's voice
'alcachofas alcachofas' it's my fine Madrid smouldering
open to all the winds
which reminds me—long years—of sea anemones
it's a head of a king's son whore's son
it's a head it's a wave which breaks
it's on the road of sea stars however
that hands are open
they don't talk of beauty of splendour
nothing but the reflections of minute skies
and the imperceptible blinkings of eyes around
the broken waves
sea-robbers
but it's Madrid open to all the winds
which tramples the word in my head
'alcachofas alcachofas'
cornices of taut cries

open up eternal heart
to enter the road of stars
in your life countless like the sand
and the seas' joy
may it hold the sun

in your breast where the man of tomorrow shines
the man of today on the road of sea stars
has planted the forward flag of life
as it should be lived
the bird's flight freely chosen until death
and until the end of stones and ages
eyes fixed on the only certainty in the world
from which light streams skimming the ground

from the inner face

2 (an extract)

hard street pavements won't you put steel steps
in my ready braced purpose to brave the winds
and the tides of mud the naked tears of cruelty
age of shamelessness
hands soiled through having drawn purity
from its radiant path lined with lavender
soiled memories shining like gold
sold to the highest bidder lies cowardices
pavements ring louder in my blind breast
and won't your hard echoes answer my grief

may my rejection of the world be of stone
hatred my answer sweet death my only friend
and depth you loneliness of my oblivion among things and beings

so spoke the man in the middle of the path
and I heard the slow suns of voices
that skirted the stone the shadow and the ashes
the blood of the unvanquished

I've heard the protest I've seen people pass
bowed uncaring under the rain's deafness
each one carried within himself part of the light
curbed joys and put blinkers on sufferings

oh lives humiliated enveloped in anguish
your wounds wound me your knifing looks
revive defeated lives for you humiliated
I carry the old old shame of living without blushing

from door to door I carry the shame and hatred
shadow for this earth death matures in me
its crystal seeds set in my memory
its blurred reflections stab life in its hope

is there still laughter I've half-opened the door
where youth throws us past alms
the room always filled with sun clusters
that grief shares amongst the town's poor

I've still said nothing I flee between my fingers
my life has passed beyond the murderous expectation
of my desire a blind slender flame
runs from eye to eye and kills each evening's autumn

so spoke the man in the middle of his field
all around the grass was going to milk the last rays' gleam
and wisdom awakened like a sucking newborn baby
was scattered in the air which weighed heavy
heavy with a hardly bearable richness

but the slow suns of his voice rolled on the ground
among the peaches and lucerne
they were old and faithful friendships

brothers grains of sand or millet and laburnum
sun-soaked brothers unwinding their newborn sureness
on the surface of the thin window-pane of absence
to each fate its shadow and to guard each tomb a hand
in me there's only absence
I was nowhere

I don't know you said to the clear soul
the one about which we speak where the word is king
and about which we shall speak as long as there'll be light
for those lost sight of and the serene innocence

lone clarity lone which condemns you to live
the rain shut you in
your blood burnt out
the worm of misery screws on you're far

you for a long time fastened round my anger
snake of mariner's cards on the playgrounds of legends
steeped in the wild perfumes with instructions to follow
white as purity bled by the spear of thunderbolts

your eyes still follow me
right next to mine truer than the light
their corn holds holidays that the sun doesn't know about
plains raised on the sea's glory

I've seen the slow suns of voices roll on the ground
I was nowhere

ambling along

the glance's sand
the loose earth
the tower's bark
the exchange of pleasant hills

the first stone
charming octopus
the vines torn off
from the flock of stacks
they're lying

then the low trusting water
and night everywhere
doors banging
unseen hands

the grass sheathed
the voice blocked
the road beheaded
the house buried

everything for you you see
you don't see anything anymore

acceptance of spring

I tell of a new glowing age
and a freshness turned blue
in the gold of heavy waters
set with slow blades
the doors are open ivory of ripe fruits
I tell of constancy
breasts bleed
they offer themselves to the majesty of the night

in the torn heart
waiting becomes a fire
of pigmy suns soothe the crystal tongues
those who leave devoured by their echo
but the pulse of blood
among the polished tears
at the unbelieving springs†
shares the voices the just and the strong

I tell of these springs†
that the secret of a woman's hands
has known how to keep whole
at the end of their glowing embers
what matters their brightness
if they lose their way
wander beneath the ashes
cover themselves in the fervent faith of silence

they can only tell of
dull glimmerings
wounds deeper
than sleeping countries
of which I tell—sand—
has no name in this world
where spring wrenches itself free
in great handfuls from the vanquished night

why haven't I unknown powers
light spells
grafted the fragile life
to the fierce laughter of the mountains
where old memories of fallow lands
sleep in my flesh
hear outside the immensity
burst in the trees

the fruit of castanets
is lit up in the waterfall
you revive the hidden fire
in the deceitful dawn
here are the set winds
in the robes of sleeping women
dance the night of stern ages oh stones
the numbers and their obvious victims here on earth
until the burst of bloody laughter
that earth is on earth
and increases the seed of its reign

---

† 'springs' ('sources' in the French) of water, not the season

from strays

3

I fondly recall
the wool of a childhood
hand in hand
my voice lost

may the opaque morning
take me as a root
I lose my eyes
through the eyes of leaves

I've left my childhood
to other children
those you'll laugh with
openly

I'll laugh last
deaf and alone
take me by the hand
of soft wool

4

beautiful lonely the wilderness on your lips
consider the future of doors
where escapes are entangled
the crystals of shifting hungers

the balls in their centre
the wolves busy with their winter
despair between their paws

but of all those misunderstood
you are alone in your delight

only your hands are grieving
they weep the dew of fields
the past of their gaze
holds the needle on the edge of tears
nothing appeases the sleek fire
nor extinguishes it at the tips of your fingers

lonely lonely lonely wool
where the escapes are caught

6

what do you know about it the air turns away from us
we are there without stars
what do you know about it without money without a home
a wet dog in its kennel
and the rain in your armpits
what do you know about it the noise lies
and dies with each surprise
the goods of spring
there they are coming from afar
a bottle set on the white linen
and the zinc on the counter
what do you know about it it's the ambulance laugh
he looks like a student
carts carts the key's in the door
what do you know about it fed up to the teeth with work
proclaim the maize
one mouthful comes after the other
and death stings us your arse
what do you know about it braying with black laughter

freed from returning
there you are on the right road

For Robert Desnos

in the white of my thoughts
a blackbird howls the grass sings
over the headless town
the sudden wind sighs with the blood
that shakes the seasoned tree
begging for light

Miss would you
and death shows her watch
a bracelet of empty teeth
and bones of a thousand witnesses
Miss would you
the dead wood of strong jaws
softly comes last

at the head only one hope
in the head a forest
through the breaking stars
I've known the melody
that stirs the memory
there's no more resounding voice
in Paris paved with leaves
a summer misses the summons
I'm alone in knowing it

forget your sons your mothers
youth springs
lovers' kisses
golden times
a stark name flutters again
at night round the lamps
and the clenched fist of the towns

reaches up to the heart of the day
this light this revolt
that's offered to passers-by
in the palm of the hand
of the world

in the arms that the waves bear away
a bird nothing more except anger
a face at my window
a joy floats
my secret my ambition
and the world

on account

in the Arabia of three noons
towers with cayman fronts
in the Arabia of your fresh skin
and turbans of black dreams
fire rings in the bells
sweet is the water's word
under the key of light nights
enchained in girls' hearts

fire licks the mirrors
the noses of sleepers
burn under the gaze split
in the morning's orange

it's for these tupenny-ha'penny countries
that memory empties itself
for the snow and flame
with which the stars adorn themselves

under the blind mane
runs the unquenched fire
the living crystal of springs
in the waters of the future

go my child sleep my horse
there's not enough peace
in the just hands of summits
to cover the voice of towns

without striking a blow

(an extract)

don't shoot the pianist
I've done what I could
let me also describe the vast prairie of my grape days
and the doomed wine of years that here's
herds of zincmen skewered on a single belief
with lolling tongues aspects of fear
before the sea of disasters
noon explodes in the darkness of its strength
and absurd laughter shams the joy of returns

I believed I saw my freedom in the turbulent water
although late in the day untouchable mistress
who with all your life sewed a dress of visions
I've followed your arguments what does it matter a fine caravel
carried within myself the promise of the future diamond
at the height of certainty
with the faith to live

an ocean of salt swarms at my door
the magnet closed up by too many fallen
trampled on shamed days dark iron storms
among the rains of insects a single hour strikes
in a broken breast of fine flour bread
what festival breaks on this vast world
breast broken in the dead flank of maize
so that silence fires a man's sleep
the hard insensibility to be absent

let the slender grass ripen at your windows
haven't you heard the evening shout in a whisper
halt halt no one may pass
shadows quartered
under the heavy imprints fixed to the cinder wall
have crucified the night
without body or stars without voice or end
adrift
a mist fish cut through and through
dissolves the forest where our hands clench

from the destroyed days

4

may he talk again what's he secretly saying about the waves
he says just like a word perforated swollen in his head
the world of the explosion seized its bush
here and there cut by a window
where light licks the joy of children

he's taken man back to his roots he said and it's the wind
he said guiding it through the alleyway's blindness
it's a matter of his first steps a slow waltz
goes through it from head to toe
through bursts of holes the ravines start to dance
that's where the reins begin the sound's water breaks
in fits and starts the window-panes march past the trees' slaps
a thousand dogs lap the night fall raids
peruse the immensities of mountains
behind their calm what is there except the hungry letter
bruised torn a new clairvoyance
a clearness of silence shivering on the velvet of strongholds
the void dazzled by a fiery ripple
such is night in the mountains

the weight of the world

(an extract)

I struggle on
the anger the happiness admitted
day for day and tooth for tooth
here's the hour that stirs
night strikes
these are the clogs of those who set out
to sea to batter the waves with the weight of their bodies
with their fists with all their faith in life
upset the depthless drawers
their truth has no price
it's the open laughter
it urges on the daring of the world
it causes the mountains of light
torn from the seaweed's evasive kisses
to climb to the light
it's the armed song on the fringes of light
there is only one man to hear
at the height of the brawl
tender cry of the babe-in-arms
the future to cry still louder
and the flashing waves
pile up the mounting clarities
surrounded by a thousand promised languages
joy I could foretell you
reinvent your dazzle
until your image on earth
was hidden from me under the dregs of grimaces
the stinking rags of death

I struggle on
I've seen lost eyes the war
beseeching eyes turned away from the war
wide-eyed the war
cowardly eyes low ignoble eyes
the eyes of little girls lovers
and mothers
but don't talk anymore of mothers' eyes
their brightness has forever
dulled the brightness of ours
they've watched wall of silence
for the fishermen's return
their foreheads pressed to the window-panes
the storm burst out at sea
a champagne cork lightning fastener
the lightning all along the body of a naked woman
standing on the edge of the horizon
the champagne gushes out
it's a festival free for all
the bass drum setting the earth afloat
jump who can
turn turn each one
the storm around you
there are all kinds of people
one's broken the bank
another's dandled the little girly
on his knee
the little dancer you know the little girly
the grand life at last the grand
the grandest is so obvious
while one by one the ships fall
on their knees
it's better than at the slaughterhouse
bodies tossed about
like flies

arms torn off
endless tears
coffins
faces without noses I don't know what without mouths without ears
put that back in order for me
and get on with it
at your command general
deaths in shreds deaths for nothing
comic deaths easy deaths
why haven't they waited for the grand dance
that's coming here
hardly noticeable
button warfare closures lightning
neon warfare hesitation waltz
death by laughing
forward the music
dead people in lace
mangled packed liquefied
tossed on the rubbish-heap
what does the fitting song matter
love song sad song life song
at your command general
there's no possible song left
love tossed in the dustbin
suppression of sorrows cure
by the release of closures lightning
you don't have to say it
it's a frenzied dance
block-head
I ask you
it's the expressive waltz
block-head
devil's brass-foundry
hag-head
you want to laugh
automatic release

whore-head
billiard-head
headline pig-head
king-head mule-head
the war above our heads
what
the war
who's being fooled
I struggle on
I've seen the horror engraved right on the retinas
of those who by wanting to survive
have died a thousand times at the back of their eyes friends
the bottom of a sea shows all the memories
bottom of grief
the dreams flow round there green cavalcades
with long strands of seaweed
deep is the breath of the wind between the rocks
and long long the history of tortures
I struggle on
the night is long
the story for the rest of us
soon reaches its end
will we have stopped believing in grief
we must take life
as it is again
face to face
good and evil
always as a comrade
shaking it from head to toe
or talking to it gently
according to what it says according to what it thinks
take it round the waist
shake it like a plum tree
and perhaps we will have to fight
so that some life is left us comrades
that each one finds his share

filled with dreams sown with childhoods
the first clarity
common to all and which has no name

the corn is still not ripe
stalks paler than thistles
in the autumn wind

the vineyard still lies fallow
man has laid his greatness
at the foot of the abyss

the sun prepares peaceful fellings
the forests will pale
with an explosive thirst for greenery

where are you newborn youth
the crimson flowers of youth
on your delicate cheeks

like the seagull's lost cry
I've lost you
the wind the night

it's true I struggle on
but in each laughing face
appears apple of my eye
my love
the present and future love
the weight of the world

from Good Time

2

blighted fruits
jagged walls
dead snow
polluted hours
locked steps
have broken up the streets
the disgrace of living
floods my eyes

furnaces dead
toothless laughter
squares trampled
harassed old-age
outlined in the hearth
all the misery
in order to tread on
the disembowelled horses
in the arena of heads
shutters stolen
open houses
children outside
straw words
as the only truth

empty mattress
no use for sleeping
or laughing or dreaming
cold in your guts
iron in the snow
burning in your throat

what have you done what have you done
hands warm with tenderness
have you lost the heaven
in your head through the world
in the stone in the wind
friendship and the smile
like dogs run wild
like dogs

Full Gas

(an extract)

a thousand years a thousand years went by and that was only a night
a little more a little less is surely and deeply
swallowed up on the way I don't know what the past
today's worry leads me on

let's always go further back
to Zurich in the haze of adolescence
I see myself hatch in the egg light
of my youth
the war was raging the road revolved
I revolved wild songless record
life revolved around me flapping its wings
was I a lion in a cage or a wood-sparrow
and what was urging on out of desire this courage in me
through the cry of that day that rejoins my steps
I discovered love
a sharp feeling that no one can name
doubles my grief underlines the wake
unlimited question an indifferent breath
keeps my unruly existence up on the surface
the waves plotted the ship's loss
and all was sworn in order to let her sink
a thousand years a thousand years went by the lightning on a
            summer's day
virgins sacrificed under the myth's whiteness
has anyone discoursed on their mad wisdom
weapons dedicated to the vanities of doubt
I'm going to meet a naked innocence
I'm at the cross-roads of my confused years

I'll never say enough the gentle power
the velvety feel of slightly muffled sentences
Paul I think of you nurse of the stars
my youth flowed then without security
rue du Cherche-Midi and rue Ordener
we searched for twelve o'clock when it struck fourteen o'clock
in the great boulevards at the exits of office-buildings
boys and girls leaving hugging one another
beauty struck me in the face like a slap in the face
I didn't know where to look
young girls flocked on all sides at once
showing all spring in their hair
there were tall ones redheads and brunettes
and they were all beautiful
the beauties of yesterday today are grandmothers
and through their wrinkles there's only me who knows how
to rediscover the charm written in their laughter
the bitter dust of sleeping dreams

what would I say of the nights we drank in peace
hours all too short feverish sowings
suddenly caught in concentric floods
Paris my fine torment on the flowering embankments
at the waters crossroads flags flapping
all those fourteenth julys in sharp flashes
I remember the grey mornings slowly passing
a ship in the harbour of our arms
I've embraced life at its surest roots
faithful I've multiplied my kept promises

end of summer

a heavy love covered in moss
shares the gold of my thoughts
barrel where memory rings
drunkennesses dreams cloudy nights

the sharp sage rouses it
and the fennel mocks it
it pours madness into the wind
where its hair's water sinks

but had madness or sweetness
turned things upside down in my head
it's in turn a single affliction
that comes and goes from day to day

Sources

Where possible the exact year of composition is given, or the years between which the poem is known to have been written. The title and publication date of the first collection in which the poem appeared is then given.

evening / soir (written 1913) published: *De nos oiseaux* (1929)

Cosmic Realities Vanilla Tobacco Dawnings / Réalités Cosmiques Vanille Tabac Eveils (written 1914) published: *De nos oiseaux* (1929)

The Dada Review / La Revue Dada (written 1916) published: *De nos oiseaux* (1929)

The Jugglers / Les Saltimbanques (written 1916) published: *De nos oiseaux* (1929)

The Seaman / Le Marin (written 1916) published: *De nos oiseaux* (1929)

Circus / Cirque (written 1917) published: *De nos oiseaux* (1929)

total circuit by the moon and colour / circuit total par la lune et par la couleur (written 1917) published: *De nos oiseaux* (1929)

the death of guillaume apollinaire / la mort de guillaume apollinaire (written 1918) published: *De nos oiseaux* (1929)

cinema calendar of the abstract heart / cinéma calendrier du coeur abstrait (written 1918) published: *Cinéma calendrier du coeur abstrait. Maisons* (1920)

maison flac / maison flake (written 1918) published: *Cinéma calendrier du coeur abstrait. Maisons* (1920)

railway station / gare (written 1916-18) published: *Vingt-cinq poèmes* (1918)

the white leprous giant in the countryside / le géant blanc lépreux du paysage (written 1916–18) published: *Vingt-cinq poèmes* (1918)

the great lament over my obscurity / la grande complainte de mon obscurité (written 1916–18) published: *Vingt-cinq poèmes* (1918)

drugstore-conscience / droguerie-conscience (written 1916–18) published: *Vingt-cinq poèmes* (1918)

small town in siberia / petite ville en sibérie (written 1916–18) published: *Vingt-cinq poèmes* (1918) instant our brother / instant notre frère (written 1916–18) published: *Vingt-cinq poèmes* (1918)

glass to pass through peaceful / verre traverser paisible (written 1916–18) published: *Vingt-cinq poèmes* (1918)

retreat / retraite (written 1916–18) published: *Vingt-cinq poèmes* (1918)

springtime / printemps (written 1916–18) published: *Vingt-cinq poèmes* (1918)

notes / remarques (written 1916-18) published: *Vingt-cinq poèmes* (1918)

dada song / chanson dada (written 1921) published: *De nos oiseaux* (1929)

on a sun-ripple / sur une ride du soleil (written 1922) published: *De nos oiseaux* (1929)

vegetable swallow / hirondelle végétale (written 1922) published: *De nos oiseaux* (1929)

around / autour (written 1922) published: *De nos oiseaux* (1929)

the condemned / le condamné (written 1923) published: *L'arbre des voyageurs* (1930)

Mr AA the antiphilosopher / Monsieur AA l'antiphilosophe (written 1916–24) published: *L'antitête* (1933)

landscapes and accidents / paysages et accidents (written 1923) published: *L'arbre des voyageurs* (1930)

Way / Voie (written 1924–25) published: *Indicateur des chemins de coeur* (1928)

Approach / Accès (written 1924–25) published: *Indicateur des chemins de coeur* (1928)

Volt / Volt (written 1924–25) published: *Indicateur des chemins de coeur* (1928)

Rule / Règle (written 1924–25) published: *Indicateur des chemins de coeur* (1928)

Palm Grove / Palmeraie (written 1929) published: *A perte de nuages* (1930)

The approximate man / L'homme approximatif (written 1925–30, published: 1931)

budding traps / pièges en herbe (written 1930) published: *Où boivent les loups* (1932)

where the wolves drink / où boivent les loups (written 1931) published: *Où boivent les loups* (1932)

the well-digger of looks / le puisatier des regards (written 1932) published: *Où boivent les loups* (1932)

night summary / abrégé de la nuit (written 1934) published: *Midis gagnés* (1939)

on the road of sea stars / sur le chemin des étoiles de mer (written 1935–36)
   published: *Midis gagnés* (1939)

the inner face / la face intérieure (written 1937–42, published: 1953)

ambling along / cheminant (written 1943–45) published: *Terre sur terre* (1946)

acceptance of spring / acceptation du printemps (written 1943–45) published:
   Terre sur terre (1946)

strays / égarées (written 1945) published: *Parler seul* (1950)

For Robert Desnos / Pour Robert Desnos (written 1946) published: *Le fruit
   permis* (1956)

on account / pour compte. Published in *Phases* (1949)

without striking a blow / sans coup férir (published: 1949)

the destroyed days / le temps détruit. Published: *De mémoire d'homme* (1950)

the weight of the world / le poids du monde. Published: *De mémoire d'homme*
   (1950)

Good Time / La bonne heure (published: 1955)

Full Gas / A haute flamme (published: 1955)

end of summer / fin d'un été. Published: *Le temps naissant* (1955)

dada / My Heart Belongs to Dada

an essay by
Lee Harwood

1 Preface

It's an evening early in the spring of 1916. In a shabby side street in Zurich is a small bar. Here there is a cabaret—the Cabaret Voltaire.

Outside Zurich and neutral Switzerland is the ceaseless carnage of the First World War. In the German offensive at Verdun in between March and September there are 395,000 French casualties and 405,000 German. This is to be followed by the British offensive on the Somme where between July and November the casualties are 400,000 British and 260,000 German. The 'blood bath' fills up and the bishops bless the guns.

Inside the cabaret a group of young men and women, poets and painters, exiles and refugees from the war, perform. Around the walls of the bar are pictures by Hans Arp, Viking Eggeling, Marcel Janco, Macke, Marinetti, Modigliani, Nadelmann, Pablo Picasso, and many others. 'Coloured papers, ascendancy of the New Art, abstract art and geographic futurist map-poems.'[1] On the small stage the performers recite poems, shout manifestos, sneer and strut and charm, sing, dance, and make music.

Tristan Tzara, Richard Huelsenbeck and Marcel Janco perform a 'simultaneous poem'. All three recite together in three different languages—French, English and German—texts that have nothing to do with one another and are a mixture of poetry, sentimental popular songs, pompous and boring letters and journals, nonsense, and pure and meaningless sounds. And all this is interspersed with the beating of a giant drum, whistles being blown, laughter and lots of rrrrrrrrrrrrrr.

This explosion is followed by 'Negro' songs. The words sung or chanted and all accompanied by 'big and small exotic drums'.[2] The texts themselves are sometimes taken from German anthropology magazines and then treated by Tzara, or sometimes totally invented and interspersed with mumbo-jumbo.

Then Hugo Ball, in a costume made of tubes of cardboard, is carried on stage and intones—

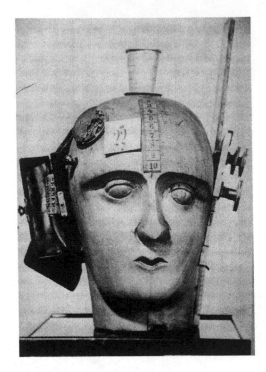

Raoul Hausman,
Wooden Head, 1918

gadji beri bimba
glandridi lauli lonni cadori
gadjama bim beri glassala
glandridi glassala tuffm i zimbrabim
blassa galassa tuffm i zimbrabim...[2]

Ball wears a tight-fitting cylinder of shiny blue cardboard with two more blue tubes for his legs. Over this is a huge coat collar, again cut out of cardboard. It's scarlet inside and gold outside and is fastened at the neck so that by raising or lowering his elbows it could flap like a pair of wings. And on his head he wears a high blue and white striped witch doctor's hat. As he continues to chant—

zimzim urallala zimzim urallala zimzim zanzibar...[3]

—some of the audience begins to protest, some laugh and applaud. Ball continues, unable to move because of his costume.

There is piano music and balalaika music. Emmy Hennings performs songs with an intentional shrillness that jars and perturbs the audience. There is 'tumult and solar avalanche.'

And all this is to be called DADA!
And what's DADA?

2 Apologies and Asides

As always when we turn to the Oxford English Dictionary we get a neat enough summary of what we're looking for. And so—'Dada...an international artistic movement repudiating tradition and reason, and intended to outrage.'

This is all true enough. Dadaism was a brief anarchic art movement that started in Zurich and lasted from 1916 to 1923 at the latest. For many people, and even those interested in the history of art, that's it. They might add that it's considered the first 'anti-art' movement as well as the father of Surrealism. But after such generalizations the details blur and the trouble begins. The trouble is in how we can come to an understanding of the very special and particular qualities this movement represents. The Dada movement was filled with contradictions and complexities and it's only too easy to be distracted by the historical chronology of Dadaism and to miss the essence of Dada.

To get a clear idea of Dada some wider issues must be considered if we're to avoid approaching it as an irrelevant though colourful antique. We also need to get past some of our present prejudices. Dada, as I've said, is considered the first 'anti-art' movement and these days there is nothing more art conscious than 'anti-art' movements. 'Anti-art' groups depend for their effect, their power to shock or impress, on their audience having firm preconceptions of the nature of art and their being knowledgeable about contemporary art and art history. Marcel Duchamp's *Mona Lisa* with a moustache drawn on is fairly meaningless if you don't know the original portrait by Leonardo da Vinci. In recent years the whole concept of a self-conscious avant-garde, especially 'anti-art,' has been rightly questioned and criticized for the narrow and incestuous art it often produces. It has become very much a matter of the children of the middle class denouncing and provoking the middle class, and a lot of money being made out of the whole game by dealers, artists, and critics. But writing this now is a far cry from the world of 1916. Whereas you can be rightly cynical about some expres-

Francis Picabia, Title page for *'Dada' no. 4 / 5*, 1918

Cover, *Dada no. 6*, edited by Tristan Tzara, Paris, 1920

sions of contemporary avant-garde art, it is unjust to apply the same cynicism to the events that took place eighty-five years ago. What is quite undeniable about Dada is that it was a movement outstanding in its energy and freshness and the intense sense of urgency that drove it forward while the need was there. The fact that the 'anti-art' approaches of the Dadaists have since been grossly debased can in no way detract from the worth of the original Dadaists. As proof of this, if proof be needed, one only has to look at the many great artists who participated in this movement. Max Ernst, Hans Arp, George Grosz, Kurt Schwitters and Tristan Tzara are only a few of the names whose artistic careers included a full involvement with Dada.

There is another issue to be considered before I go further, though it is maybe of a more personal and embarrassing nature. If you feel a great sympathy and enthusiasm for Dadaism, as I do, then the act of writing this article is a contradiction in itself. There are some justly chastening lines in Allen Ginsberg's poem *Howl*—

I saw the best minds of my generation destroyed by madness, starving
　　hysterical naked...
...
who threw potato salad at CCNY lecturers on Dadaism and
　　subsequently presented themselves on the granite steps of
　　the madhouse with shaven heads and harlequin speech of suicide,
　　demanding instantaneous lobotomy,

and who were given instead the concrete void of insulin
    metrasol electricity hydrotherapy psychotherapy
    occupational therapy pingpong and amnesia...[4]

While echoing the earlier anguish and rage of the Dadaists Ginsberg also includes this prickly question. How does one reconcile trying to explain a truly radical arts group that really wanted to tear things down, do something new, and to destroy all rigid and programmed thought? A group that was against all previous explanations, against all explanations? As Tristan Tzara said, quoting Descartes, 'I do not even wish to know if there were men before me.'

This contradiction, of course, goes beyond my immediate predicament back to the Dadaists themselves. By now it's a sad fact that 'radical' art groups become institutionalized by history and art critics and the artists themselves. It happened to the Dadaists and is now happening to the Beat Generation writers with learned studies and biographies of Allen Ginsberg and Jack Kerouac. There is the unedifying sight of the quarrels between the Dadaists, or ex-Dadaists, in later years. Who discovered the word 'dada' for example? Was it Tzara or was it Ball and Huelsenbeck? As Tzara ominously wrote in one of his Dada manifestos in 1918—

> We have had enough of cubist and futurist academics. Is the goal of art to earn money and to fondle the nice bourgeois? Rhymes jingle the same sound as coins, and inflexions slide along the profile of the belly. Every group of artists has finally arrived, astride various comets, at the bank, the door opened to the possibility of wallowing in cushions and rich food.[5]

3 Towards a Definition

> I write a manifesto and I want nothing, yet I say certain things, and in principle I am against manifestos, as I am also against principles...
> We are a furious wind, tearing the dirty linen of clouds and prayers, preparing the great spectacle of disaster, fire, decomposition...
> If I cry out — Ideal Ideal Ideal
>   Knowledge Knowledge Knowledge
>   Boomboom Boomboom Boomboom

I have given a pretty faithful version of progress, law, morality and all other fine qualities that various highly intelligent men have discussed in so many books…

Freedom: Dada Dada Dada, a roaring of tense colours, and interlacing of opposites and of all contradictions, grotesques, inconsistencies; LIFE.[5]

(from Tristan Tzara's *Dada Manifesto* 1918)

What was Dada? Foremost it was a violent reaction by various artists, painters and poets, to the First World War and to the society and leaders that caused that war. The organizer of the Cabaret Voltaire, Hugo Ball, wrote in his diary—

What we are celebrating is both buffoonery and a requiem mass. Our cabaret is a gesture. Every word that is spoken and sung here says at least one thing: that this humiliating age has not succeeded in winning our respect. What could be respectable and impressive about it? Its cannons? Our big drum drowns them. Its idealism? That has long been a laughing-stock, in its popular and its academic form… What we call dada is a farce of nothingness in which all higher questions are involved; a gladiator's gesture, a play with shabby leftovers, the death warrant of posturing morality and abundance.

The dadaist fights against the agony and the death throes of this age.[2]

The protests and works of the Dadaists were for them the one sane answer any artist could make to a world apparently gone insane. A feeling that absurdity and confusion must be carried further and further until everything breaks down into a silence from which a new vision can be constructed. As Ball wrote in his *Kritik*—'Perhaps it is necessary to have resolutely, forcibly produced chaos before an entirely new edifice can be built on a changed basis of belief.'[6]

At the risk of repetition it is probably best to also quote from Huelsenbeck's *En Avant Dada,* maybe the most direct and understandable account of the beginnings of Dada.

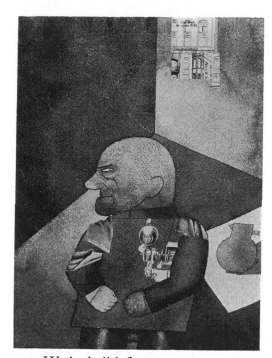

George Grosz,
The Engineer Heartfield, 1920

We had all left our countries as a result of the war. We were agreed that the war had been contrived by the various governments for the most autocratic, sordid and materialistic reasons; we Germans were familiar with the book *J'accuse*, and even without it we would have had little confidence in the decency of the German Kaiser and his generals. Ball was a conscientious objector, and I had escaped by the skin of my teeth from the pursuit of the police myrmidons who, for their so-called patriotic purposes, were massing men in the trenches of Northern France and giving them shells to eat. None of us had much appreciation for the kind of courage it takes to get shot for the idea of a nation which is at best a cartel of pelt merchants and profiteers in leather, at worst a cultural association of psycho-paths who, like the Germans, marched off with a volume of Goethe in their knapsacks, to skewer Frenchmen and Russians on their bayonets.

Tristan Tzara wrote in 1947 when looking back on Dada—

> We proclaimed our disgust… This war was not our war… Dada was
> born from an urgent moral need, from an implacable desire to attain
> a moral absolute, from the deep feeling that man, at the centre of
> all creations of the spirit, must affirm his supremacy over notions
> emptied of all human substance, over dead objects and ill-gotten
> gains… Honour, Country, Morality, Family, Art, Religion, Liberty,
> Fraternity, I don't know what, all these notions had once answered
> to human needs, now nothing remained of them but a skeleton of
> conventions, they had been divested of their initial content.[8]

Certainly the Dadaists were not the only artists to protest at the insa-
nities and inhumanities of the First World War. The German Expressionist
poets and British poets like Wilfred Owen, Isaac Rosenberg and Siegfried
Sassoon were only a few of the artists to register their dismay at the times.
While Kipling may strut on the battlefield and French Academicians stoke
up an hysterical nationalism there were these quiet and not-so-quiet voices
to gainsay them no matter how unpopular they might be in a time of flags
and white feathers. But it is the form the Dada protest took that distinguis-
hes it from the others. It was a mixture of outraged polemic and a turning to
intentional absurdity that involved an almost childlike love of games, chance,
and the fantastical. It was a strange marriage of opposites, the rage and then
a fascination with simple pleasures, with 'the daily miracle,' that turned their
backs on that rage. And both of these goals were pursued with an obsessive
energy and diversity unequalled elsewhere.

It is only by understanding the background and foundations of Dada—the
war and all that it meant—that one can move on to the particulars and see
the real meaning of the actions and works of the Dadaists. Obviously it isn't
that crude an equation of cause and effect. The Dadaists certainly developed
a number of concerns that were in the air before the war—like the interest in
African art and 'primitive art,' the performances and provocative techniques of
the Italian Futurists, and a favouring of the irrational rather than nineteenth
century scientific materialism as an explanation of wholeness—but the necessity
that drove them came from the war.

4 The Places and Events

Zurich

The Dada movement was international, it's true, and had many members and locations, but it was here in Zurich that it was named, that the first Dada magazines were published and the first manifestos proclaimed. In 1916 Switzerland was the home of numerous refugees and exiles. In Zurich lived James Joyce who'd fled from Trieste, Lenin and Zinoviev from Russia, and of course the future Dadaists such as Tristan Tzara and Marcel Janco from Rumania, Hugo Ball, Emmy Hennings, Richard Huelsenbeck and Hans Richter from Germany, and Hans Arp from Alsace. It's not surprising that out of such an international melting pot something should happen.

What did happen was Cabaret Voltaire. Hugo Ball, a poet, musician and philosopher, and the singer Emmy Hennings persuaded the owner of the Hollandische Meierei bar to allow them to present a nightly cabaret with 'artistic entertainments.' On 5 February the room was decorated with Futurist posters, the poet Tzara and the painters Arp and Janco appeared in response to a newspaper appeal by Ball, and the cabaret began. What the audience of Swiss students, solid bourgeoisie and art lovers, and foreign exiles received for their entrance money was the sort of performance already described. In mid-February the poet Huelsenbeck joined them and the group was near complete. The performances grew from being merely bizarre to a total wildness. Nothing was planned too carefully and the cabaret was often an amazing mixture of contrasts. The provocations and 'experimental' events would be interspersed with a balalaika orchestra organized by the Russians in the audience, by folk songs and dances, readings of French and German poetry, and the playing of Liszt's thirteenth Hungarian Rhapsody!

The cabaret was finally closed on 23 June 1916 after complaints from the public to the owner of the bar. But a movement had started, been established, that would not disintegrate until 1923. Exactly how this movement was eventually named, after its loose and spontaneous beginnings, we shall never know. The word DADA was picked at random from a dictionary and, according to Ball, was first used in the April of that year, and that is but one of the many conflicting reports. We do know the word first appeared in print on 15 June 1916.

While Hugo Ball was organizer of the early events, it was Tzara who became the driving force behind the Dada publications and, as a result,

Hans Arp, Woodcut

Dada publicity. Through their magazines, books and anthologies the Zurich group made their international contacts and the Dada movement spread as a conscious entity. Dada grew like a crystal, though not so slowly and sedately. The cabaret events, then the publications and all the letters between artists that resulted from these, then the exhibitions, then the visits to Zurich by other artists like Francis Picabia, then the travels of the original Dadaists.

An incomplete summary of the Dada publications would begin in June 1916 with *Cabaret Voltaire,* an anthology edited by Ball. It included work by Apollinaire, Arp, Cendrars, Huelsenbeck, Kandinsky, Marinetti, Modigliani, Picasso and Tzara. This was followed by a series of illustrated books of poetry edited by Tzara, the series titled *Collection Dada.* Then between 1917 and 1921 Tzara edited the magazine *Dada* which ran to seven issues. The second issue, for example, contained work by Arp, Birot, de Chirico, Kandinsky, and many others. And in 1919 Tzara co-edited a one-shot magazine, *Der Zeltweg,* with work by Arp, Giacometti, Schwitters, and others.

With the end of Cabaret Voltaire and the publication of Ball's anthology Dada moved into a new phase. It started on a series of more consci-

At Weimar, 1922. From left to right: Hans Richter, Tristan Tzara, Jean Arp.

ously public activities. The group of friends at the beginning had come together almost spontaneously and produced the cabaret, but with time the whole
affair became more self-conscious. The act of giving itself a name was in a way a
step nearer Dada's becoming one more artistic organization, an aim far from the
original intentions of the group. This inevitably caused tensions within the group,
especially between the two chief figures Ball and Tzara. Ball was nervous of the
way things were developing while Tzara could only see them with enthusiasm.

On 14 July the first public Dada soirée was held at the Waag Hall in Zurich.
This evening, which included the reading of manifestos by Arp, Ball, Janco,
Huelsenbeck and Tzara, ended in a near riot, according to Tzara. Immediately
after this Ball left Zurich, and at the beginning of 1917 Huelsenbeck also left
equally dissatisfied with the direction things were taking, though for slightly
different reasons to Ball's. Tzara, a natural propagandist and an activist very
conscious of being part of an aggressive European avant-garde, then took over
administrative leadership of the group.

In January 1917 there was a Dada exhibiton at Galerie Coray of work
by Arp, Janco, Richter and Van Kees, and a show of African art. Then
in March Ball was persuaded to return to Zurich briefly and until May he

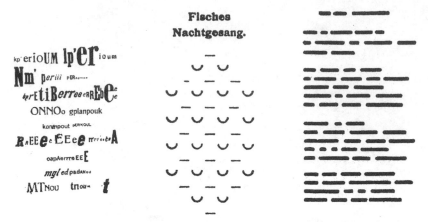

1. Raoul Hausmann, Optophonetic poem, 1918. 2. Christian Morgenstern, Phonetic poem. 3. Man Ray, Phonetic poem, 1924.

and Tzara organized Galerie Dada, using the Coray premises. The Galerie Dada showed paintings by Bloch, Baumann, de Chirico, Max Ernst, Feininger, Kandinsky, Paul Klee, Kokoschka and Modigliani, along with paintings by children, African sculptures, and various 'artifacts' including embroidery. There was a series of lectures including Ball on Kandinsky and E. Jollos on Klee. There were soirées organized around particular themes. There were performances of plays, poetry, manifestos, music and dance. They even held afternoon teas for school parties and gave guided tours of the exhibition for 'local workmen.'

After the closure of the Galerie Dada Tzara went on to organize many more Dada evenings with larger and larger audiences and with increasingly provocative and violent performances. These along with exhibitions and lectures continued until the end of the war and beyond it into 1919. The last and largest Dada soirée was held in April 1919 when, claimed Tzara, '1,500 persons filled the hall already boiling in the bubbles of bamboulas.' 'Dada has succeeded in establishing the circuit of absolute unconsciousness in the audience which forgot the frontiers of education of prejudices, experienced the commotion of the NEW.'[1]

It is not insignificant that Tzara should also write in his *Zurich Chronicle*—'1917 July. Mysterious creation! magic revolver! The DADA MOVEMENT is launched.'[1] Not only does this coincide with the first issue of *Dada* magazine but also with Ball and Huelsenbeck having left Zurich and Tzara becoming the chief director of Dada. At the heart of the matter—the division within the group mentioned earlier—is a question very pertinent to us in 2005. What Ball and Huelsenbeck were suspicious of was the way Dada was in fact creating yet another public system and style. No matter how anarchic and wild that style might become it was still a style, an orthodox stance, and it was such orthodoxies that the early Dadaists had denounced in their calls of freedom, openness and decency. Ball wrote in his diary that art was 'not an end in itself... but... an opportunity for true perception and criticism of the times' (5 June 1916).[2] For Ball and Huelsenbeck art was a means to an end. It was for this reason that Ball co-directed the Galerie Dada, because it had an educational aim. But for Tzara Dada was an end in itself, to be used then discarded when needs be.

The sequel to this is that Ball retreated first into politics, then into religion and mysticism. Huelsenbeck, moving to Berlin, devoted himself to political action, using art and Dada techniques as his weapons. And Tzara pushed forward with his concept of Dada as 'ghosts drunk on energy, we dig the trident into unsuspecting flesh,' as 'a furious wind, tearing the dirty linen of clouds and prayers,'[5] and that 'Dada is idiotic. Hurrah for Dada."[9] Dada as blatantly anti-art and an aggressively 'nihilistic' force to shake everything up. There were no plans beyond this. No plans could be made until a new consciousness existed. In its way such 'nihilism' is as constructive an act as the more self-conscious constructions of artists like Ball and Huelsenbeck. It may even be argued that it is the healthier choice, certainly at that point in history. If any folk wisdom can be found in this chronicle it must be that 'there's more ways than one to skin a cat.'

In January 1920 Tzara left Zurich for Paris. That plus the new freedom of movement that came with the end of the war meant that Zurich died as a centre of Dada activities. In its four years it had seen the rapid development of many artistic possibilities that were to spread far beyond that city. Zurich Dada has to its unique credit the development of sound poems, simultaneous poems, the use of manifestos, performance art, and Tzara's notorious cut-up poems. The recipe for this last item is: 'To make a Dadaist poem take a newspaper. Take a pair of scissors. Choose an article as long as you are planning to make your poem. Cut out the article. Then cut out each of the words that make up this article and put them in a bag. Shake it gently. Then take out the scraps one after the other. In the order in which they left the bag copy conscientiously. The poem will be like you. And here you are a writer, infinitely original and endowed with a sensibility that is charming though beyond the understanding of the vulgar.'[9] Or as Mary Ann Caws states more academically: 'For Dada, the role of poetry is to create and develop, against the closed and the prosaic a permanent atmosphere of

George Grosz, Drawing for
'*Der blutige Ernst*'

openness, of clarity, intensity, and rapidity, to which the energetic oppositions of contradictory elements is absolutely essential.'[10]

Berlin

When Huelsenbeck left Zurich in January 1917 and arrived in Berlin he moved into a very different world. It was not a matter of shocking the Swiss bourgeois—not a very difficult thing to achieve—but being right in the middle of a society in tumult and revolt, and working with that revolution which put into action what had only been words in Zurich. From 1917 onwards within the city of Berlin there was a series of mutinies by the armed forces, of street battles, political murders, soldiers' councils, workers' councils, the brief Communist takeover of Berlin, and all the hardships and cruelties that came with the ending of the First World War. Even with the establishment of the Weimar Republic in 1919 there was no end to the civil and intellectual strife.

As happened elsewhere, a group of artists had already assembled whose views and attitudes were akin to the Zurich Dadaists. It only took Huelsenbeck to read his 'First Dada Speech in Germany' in February 1918 for Berlin Dada to be officially launched. In Germany the divisions and differing qualities of the

Zurich Dada artists were to be seen on a national scale, but pushed even further and on a far greater and more ambitious scale. Berlin was to be the centre of political Dada, of the 'art with a purpose,' while Cologne and Hanover were where Dada pursued art for its own sake, but it was their own concept of art not anyone else's.

The Berlin action began. A Club Dada was formed whose most prominent members were the painters and graphic artists George Grosz, John Heartfield and Hannah Hoech, the poet and artist Raoul Hausmann, the poets Walter Mehring and Richard Huelsenbeck, and Johannes Baader, the arch demonstrator and action man of the group. But to define any of the members by the form taken by the bulk of their art is a mistake. As in Zurich, only more so, all these artists wrote manifestos, arranged meetings and performances, and tried out all the possibilities of visual images, typography, words, sounds, and action. Though the Club Dada was not above its own human weaknesses and exclusivities, despite the apparent revolutionary openness. Kurt Schwitters, for example, was refused membership for being insufficiently political and having a 'bourgeois face.'

After the founding of the Club the Berlin Dada group pursued the same course of events as Zurich but this time they were up against a real opposition, not an indulgent audience. Numerous magazines were published such as *Der blutige Ernst* (Deadly Earnest, 1919) and *Jedermann sein eigner Fussball* (Every man his own football, 1919). These were quickly banned by the authorities, but then reappeared under new titles like *Die Pleite* (Bankrupt, 1919–24). *Jedermann sein...* was charged with 'seeking to bring the Armed Forces into contempt and distributing indecent publications.'[3] Other notable publications were the magazine *Der Dada* (1919–20) and Huelsenbeck's *Dada Almanach* and his famous pamphlet *En Avant Dada*. A series of readings was arranged by Club Dada between 1918 and 1920. These were not only held in Berlin but the trio of Huelsenbeck, Hausmann and Baader travelled as far as Dresden, Hamburg and Leipzig in Germany and Prague and Teplice in the Czech Republic to deliver their mixture of enraged polemic, poetry and provoking absurdities. In Prague, despite the facts that the Czechs wanted to beat them up as they were Germans, and the Germans believed they were Bolsheviks, and the Socialists threatened them with 'death and annihilation because they regarded [them] as reactionary voluptuaries,'[7] Huelsenbeck and Hausmann won over a massive audience. Baader had fled before the performance believing 'he would end his poetic career in a Prague morgue.'[7]

The climax of the Dada events in Berlin was the 'First International Dada Fair' in June 1920. Besides paintings and graphics by the Dadaists, the centrepiece of the exhibition was a stuffed effigy of a German officer with a pig's head hung from the ceiling with a placard reading 'Hanged by the Revolution.' But possibly the ultimate act in the Berlin Dada's programme of protest with the maximum use of publicity was in 1923. This was when the poet and Dadaist Franz Jung hijacked a German freighter in the Baltic and presented it with its cargo to the Soviet authorities in Petrograd!

Though Berlin Dada had inevitably dissolved by 1923, due to the change in the times and pressures, and all the internal feuds that made the participants return to their own artistic careers, it had made its point and some major artistic work was achieved that is as fresh and powerful today as then. What is most memorable is the stunning development of photomontage by John Heartfield and also by Hausmann and Grosz. Equally outstanding was the use of typography in the Dada publications, and the further and wilder development of sound poetry by Hausmann and Huelsenbeck. At the major retrospective exhibition of Dada (and Surrealism) at the Hayward Gallery in London in 1978 it was these works that were most moving, despite the antiseptic surroundings, while much else had become merely historical documents. It's therefore curious how so many scholarly critics ignore this side of Dada and concentrate on the Paris group, a tamer and more literary affair.

Cologne

Cologne was not so much the centre for a Dada group as the home town of the artist Max Ernst. He, with the help of friends like Johannes Baargeld and Hans Arp, produced a very special form of Dada in that city. He and his paintings and collages represented the positive side of Dada. Rather than concentrate on protest, as in Berlin, he chose to develop the side of Dada we find in the primitive forms of Arp's woodcuts and the religious chants of Hugo Ball's sound poems. Ernst wanted in his art a return to the illogical, chance, magic, 'fairy stories,' the world of alarming dreams and primitive myths. His mysterious and unnerving collages are not concerned with contemporary politics but are echoes of something deeper and more eternal. Just as much as the Dada polemics of Berlin, Ernst's work was to awake and stimulate the minds of his audience but in a more subtle and long-lasting way.

Of course Dada in Cologne went through the usual paces as elsewhere. A magazine edited by Baargeld, *Der Ventilator,* was banned by the British occupation forces as being subversive in 1919. Then Ernst edited his own one-shot magazine *Die Schammade* (a combination of the German words for charade and witch-doctor) in 1920, including the Paris Dada poets Aragon, Breton and Eluard. Even a Dada Fair was put on in 1920, closed by the authorities and then reopened when the only offending work that could be found was by Albrecht Durer. The exhibition itself was made up of various disturbing objects, collages and photomontages. Entry to the fair was through the gent's toilet of a beer-hall. Added attractions were a girl dressed for her First Communion reciting obscene poems and a statue by Ernst at the entrance with an axe attached and an invitation to destroy it. From this it should be obvious that Ernst and his friends lacked neither wit nor spirit in the pursuit of their more serious aims and ambitions. The residence of Dada in Cologne ended when Ernst left for Paris in 1921. Ernst's own brand of Dada did not end there but continued and grew in his work for the rest of his life.

Hanover

Dada in Hanover was even more of a one-man show than Cologne in the person of the poet, painter and sculptor Kurt Schwitters. After his rejection by the Berlin Club Dada Schwitters returned to Hanover to make his own form of Dada, or Merz as he called it. Like Ernst he too was not interested in the destructive side of Dada but in building things anew, creating a fresh and almost innocent vision of the world. In fact well before the start of Dada in Zurich he had been making collages but with the birth of Merz he accelerated all his earlier interests. He was fascinated by everything. He would put into his collages anything that came his way—it was all precious and, as Richter said, to be 'restored to an honoured place in life by means of his art.'[3] Old bus tickets found in the street, notices and commercial flyers, small pieces of coloured paper, string, bits of wire, pieces of wood, playing cards—all could be placed and treated in his collages and paintings. His sculptures, or rather assemblies, were the same. And in his poetry he often worked by the same principles taking and rearranging phrases from public notices or newspapers in such a way as to give them a new and mysterious meaning. It's the same method that Ernst used in his collages, juxtaposing clichéd visual images to make a startling new picture.

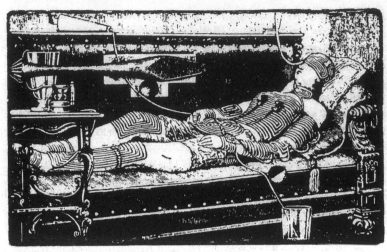

Max Ernst, *The Preparation of Glue from Bones*, 1921

Schwitters' use of these notices is seen in lines like—

> Do not open until
> the train is in motion
>
> This seat reserved for
> unhandicapped dogs.[11]

At other times he takes this further and, like Tzara's poems, collages public notices with private images. An example would be the poem *A Fourth of the Feelings of the Ancient Automato atop His Family Fortress Atho* which ends—

> When the wild wine blooms.
> Itch in my left eye.
> The calf stays dead.
> Bicycle riders are cautioned to remain in their prescribed lanes.[11]

Schwitters' sound poems are another aspect of his vision of art. While they too collage basic sounds they also are a return to primitive and direct communication. This is perhaps a too pompous description as Schwitters' wit never deserted him in these poems.

Francis Picabia,
Dada no. 7. Paris,
March 1920

Salon Dada poster

It's amazing when one considers how prolific and energetic Schwitters was. Besides all his artworks in word and image, he edited *Merz* magazine (1923–32), went on a Dada tour of Holland with Theo Van Doesburg, read in Prague with Hausmann, and gave readings in many other parts of Europe. Like *Schwitters' Column*, a sculpture that accumulatively took over two floors of Schwitters' house, *Merz* started before many other forms of Dada and went on long after them. His openness and the sense of wonder he shared with his friend Arp is best found in his statement: 'Moreover, we know that we must get rid of the idea of "Art" if we're ever going to reach "Art."'[11]

Paris

When Tristan Tzara left Zurich for Paris in January 1920 he was not just going to join and rally a group of like-minded contemporaries but to be part of a long established tradition of avant-garde art in that city. From Rimbaud, Lautréamont and Jarry right up to Apollinaire, Arthur Cravan and Jacques Vaché the Paris art world was used to provocations, and so were the public. But whereas there had previously been these individual actions and artistic groups, Tzara, in bringing the official Dada stamp to Paris, was to instigate group action and provocation on a scale never known before.

While it's easy to appreciate individual artists like Ernst and Schwitters and the more single-minded approach of Berlin Dada, it's much more difficult to grasp the special qualities of Dada in Paris. Like Zurich, Paris Dada was a much looser affair and involved a host of artists. The movement was predominantly a literary one, though various Dada painters like Ernst, Picabia and Man Ray did have exhibitions. The group of French poets associated with the magazine *Litterature*, such as André Breton, Louis Aragon and Philippe Soupault, had invited Tzara to Paris. They had been in contact with Zurich since 1917 as had Pierre Reverdy, editor of *Nord-Sud,* and Albert Birot, editor of *Sic.* Tzara's arrival took the action out of the magazines and into the streets, or rather the halls. He and Picabia gave the French poets a formula already well practised and developed in Zurich and Berlin. But the fact that it had almost become a formula was the weakness of the Dada events held in Paris between 1920 and 1922. The first Dada performance on 23 January 1920 established the ground rules of the game. The poets already mentioned along with Paul Eluard, Raymond Radiguet and Jean Cocteau read poems, read manifestos, and performed intentionally infuriating events. The audience in turn rioted and the matinée ended in pandemonium. After this both sides came prepared. The audience, often ready armed with eggs and fruit to throw at the performers, could have the 'pleasurable anticipation of a scandal,'[3] as Ribemont-Dessaignes describes it. The Dada soirées were immensely popular and, as at the Salle Gaveau on 26 May 1920, drew massive audiences. Not only were the audiences drawn by the pleasure of active participation in the evening's performance but by the general public interest in the anti-establishment ideas and humour of the Dadaists. But the repetitiveness of the events, or rather the form of the events, led to a stagnation of the movement. The result was inevitably that Dada as an active movement degenerated and fell apart leaving the ground clear for André Breton's first Surrealist Manifesto in 1924. The end of the story is not a particularly edifying one. After various failed attempts to change the course of Dada, a clear rift developed between the anarchic side represented by Tzara and Picabia and those French poets like Breton who at heart wanted a new theoretical programme. The feud culminated in a violent brawl at an event titled *Soirée du coeur à barbe* organised by Tzara on 6 July 1923. The show included Erik Satie playing some of his piano pieces, films, various recitations, and a performance of Tzara's play *Le coeur à gaz.* During a proclamation read by Pierre de Massot, Breton and his friends attacked the stage. While Breton's associates Robert Desnos and Benjamin Péret held de Massot from behind, Breton smashed him with his heavy walking stick, breaking de Massot's arm. An all-out fight followed. The police were called, some say by Tzara. And this was the end of Dada. 'There was no point in continuing,'[3] as Richter wrote in his account of those years.

New York

All the histories of Dada include a section on what they call New York Dada. Of course this depends on what definition of Dada you work by, but certainly it is a debatable question whether such a movement existed in any real sense. Dada was essentially a European movement, a reaction to particular pressures

Marcel Duchamps, *Fountain,* © ARS, NY. 1917/1964. Third version, replicated under the direction of the artist in 1964 by the Galarie Schwarz, Milan. Photo: Philippe Migeat. © 2005 Artists Rights Society (ARS), New York/ADAGP, Paris/ Succession Marcel Duchamp

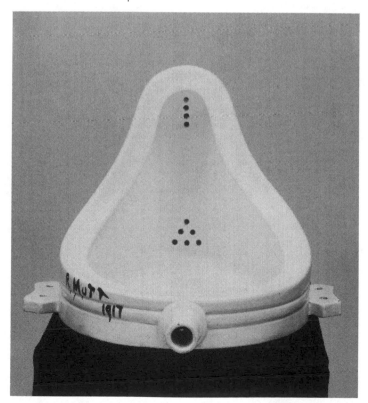

and a resulting development of current ideas and artistic techniques. Central to the claim for a New York Dada is the presence there of the French artist Marcel Duchamp from 1915 onwards. Certainly his works along with those of the American painter and photographer Man Ray show a contempt for all traditional concepts of art, as do the writings and drawings of Francis Picabia who was in New York in 1915 and 1916. And like other capital cities New York contained artists who could be associated with some aspects of Zurich Dada. But though some of the works may have had a surface resemblance to those of the Dadaists in Europe their emphasis is wholly 'anti-art' rather than anti-social. There were no events or manifestos. It all stayed safely in the studio or in the art collection of American millionaire Walter Arensberg. The only publication that could be called Dada was *New York Dada* in 1921, a four-page one-shot magazine that included a statement by Tzara and art work by Duchamp. The only time Duchamp and Ray were involved in Dada events was during their stay in Paris after the war.

Marcel Duchamp was unique as an artist. He ceased painting in 1913 and then devoted the rest of his life to creating objects and ready-mades and to playing chess. The significance of these objects and ready-mades lies in the theory behind them and it is for this that they're appreciated. They started in 1913 with the bicycle wheel mounted on a stool and continued with the bottle-rack (1914) and the notorious *Fountain* (1917), a porcelain urinal signed 'R. Mutt' submitted to the New York Independents Exhibition. Behind the act of presenting these treated and untreated articles was a cold cynicism and mockery both of art and people. There is none of the violent protest of Zurich or Berlin, nor the desire for a new vision of the world through art that Arp, Ernst and Schwitters attempted. Duchamp's cool amorality is a world apart from the passion of the European Dadaists. When we now enter the Dada sections of museums we are still moved by the paintings of Ernst, Arp, Schwitters and Grosz, despite their original proclamations against Art. Their works still have a heart while Duchamp's appear as dead objects created by a theoretically 'respectable' mind. The ready-mades no longer shock us and by their very nature don't lead us to any sense of praise for the object itself.

5 'Dada' after Dada / We're in the Money

When we view Giotto's *St. Francis Receiving the Stigmata* we obviously don't feel the same religious fervour as Giotto's contemporaries. The painting has lost that original significance and importance, and gained a new meaning for us on leaving the church and entering the museum (a relatively modern invention). We view it as art rather than propaganda. We look for colour and composition rather than a vital message. And that same fate has befallen the Dada creations. We no longer live in the same world as the Dadaists. There is not a world war on that is bringing about the collapse of the whole power and class structure of Europe. The tensions and complexities of the present times are very different to those of 1916–23. Tzara in later life rightly insisted that an artist must find new solutions for new problems. He believed that the Dada movement by its very nature had a built-in self-destruct mechanism. While he always proclaimed the need for struggle and for art to 'break the winter of things' and 'shake the laugh from the appletree,' he soundly denounced all attempts to revive Dadaism after its natural death, to invent Neo-Dada.

So what have we got from the Dada artists? What can we use from their work? The questions are easily answered if we think only in terms of artistic technique. The Dada development of photomontage, collage and experimental typography is now used in advertising, shop displays, even on record sleeves whether they be Beatles or Bach. Such is the way of the world and fashion. The surfaces are copied but not the original spirit and intentions behind them. But this certainly makes our commercial surroundings a little more interesting and lively. But when we consider the relation between Dada and contemporary art the conclusions are not so pleasing, nor so interesting. What the art critics have called Neo-Dada and Pop Art in the visual arts has been nothing more than an exploitation of Dada, a commercial exploitation that hasn't truly developed Dada ideas in any way. U.S. and even U.K. Pop Art in the 1960s and 1970s showed an uncritical fascination and acceptance of the objects and materials of a consumer society. Roy Lichtenstein really likes sentimental comic strips as Andy Warhol does packaging and Hollywood. Often it was a pure fascination with surfaces. Such glossy art works are a world apart from the violence of thought and the critical and political stands of the Dadaists. This is not anti-art but art money. And the same disease has spread to other art forms. A grisly example would be the 'happenings' arranged by the weal-

thy Parisian Jean-Jacques Lebel in the 1960s where French débutantes cla-
moured to be allowed to take part. The lessons of the 1920s about providing
fashionable scandal for the bourgeois have not been learnt. Harold Rosenberg
describes Pop Art as 'Advertising art which advertises itself as art that hates
advertising.'[3]

Of course it is not really such a depressing state of affairs. Several artists have
successfully developed Dada techniques, but they are in the minority and don't
add up to a neo-Dada movement, nor would they think of calling themselves
such. The paintings of Robert Rauschenberg have effectively and movingly used
collage. The writings of William Burroughs have developed and refined the use
of cut-up and literary collage first used by Tzara and Schwitters. And both
Rauschenberg and Burroughs have in their art made a fierce attack on authority
and power games, whether they be obvious like the Vietnam War or more subtle
like the thought control exercised by governments and the media.

When faced with the sight of a Duchamp article—a book with a foam-rub-
ber breast on the cover inscribed 'touch me'—inside a strong glass case surrounded by security guards inside a museum there is luckily an alternative to such
foolishness. It's in the words of poems by Tzara–

> on a new made horizon
> a water drapery running vast alive
> grates small special coefficient
> of my love
> in the suddenly opened door[12]

It's in the anarchic lines of Max Stirner—'rebellion is to no longer let ourselves
be arranged.'[2]

Sources

The best collection of the main Dada manifestoes and texts in translation is *The Dada Painters and Poets* edited by Robert Motherwell (Documents of Modern Art, vol. 8 / Wittenborn, Schulz, Inc., New York, 1951). Of all the books on Dada the most readable and accurate account is Hans Richter's *Dada Art and Anti-Art* (Thames & Hudson, London, 1965).

Sources of Quotations:
1 Tristan Tzara—*Zurich Chronicle 1915–19* (in *Dada Almanach*, Berlin, 1920) included in Motherwell's anthology
2 Hugo Ball—*Flight out of time* (Viking Press, New York, 1974)
3 Hans Richter—*Dada Art and Anti-Art*
4 Allen Ginsberg—*Howl & other poems* (City Lights Books, San Francisco, 1959)
5 Tristan Tzara—*Dada Manifesto 1918* (in *Sept manifestes Dada*, Jean Budry, Paris, 1924) see Motherwell
6 Hugo Ball—*Zur Kritik der deutschen Intelligenz* (Freie Verlag, Bern, 1919)
7 Richard Huelsenbeck—*En Avant Dada: A History of Dadaism* (Paul Steegemann Verlag, Hanover / Leipzig, 1920) see Motherwell
8 Tristan Tzara—*Le surréalisme et l'après-guerre* (Nagel, Paris, 1947)
9 Tristan Tzara—*Manifesto on feeble love and bitter love* (in *Sept manifestes Dada*) see Motherwell
10 Mary Ann Caws—*The poetry of Dada and Surrealism* (Princeton U.P., Princeton, 1970)
11 *Three Painter Poets: Arp, Schwitters, Klee* (Penguin Books, Harmondsworth, 1974)
12 Tristan Tzara—*Chanson Dada: Selected Poems* (Black Widow Press, Boston, 2005)

Bibliography of Tristan Tzara:
Books published 1916–1982

Poetry

1916 *La première aventure céleste de Monsieur Antipyrine.* Collection Dada, no. 1, Zurich.

1918 *Vingt-cinq poèmes.* Collection Dada. Zurich.

    1946 *Vingt-cinq-et-un poèmes.* Collection l'âge d'or, Editions de la Revue Fontaine, Paris. (1918 text augmented with an unpublished poem.)

1920 *Cinéma calendrier du coeur abstrait. Maisons.* Collection Dada, Au Sans Pareil, Paris.

1928 *Indicateur des chemins de coeur.* Editions Jeanne Bucher, Paris.

1929 *De nos oiseaux.* Editions Kra, Paris.

1930 *L'arbre des voyageurs.* Editions de la Montagne, Paris.

1931 *L'homme approximatif.* Editions Fourcade, Paris.

    1968 Second edition. Collection Poésie, NRF / Editions Gallimard, Paris.

1932 *Où boivent les loups.* Editions des Cahiers Libres, Paris.

    1968 Second edition. Poésie Club, Guy Chambelland, Librairie Saint-Germain-des-Prés, Paris.

1933 *L'antitête.* Editions des Cahiers Libres, Paris.

    1949 Second edition. Editions Bordas, Paris.

1934 *Primele Poeme ale jui Tristan Tzara urmate de Insurectia dela Zurich.* Editura Unu, Bucharest. (Tzara's first poems, written in Rumanian.)

    1965 *Les Premiers poèmes.* Editions Seghers, Paris. (French translation of the 1934 text revised by Tzara, and five unpublished early poems.)

1935 *La main passe.* Editions G.L.M., Paris.

1935 *Sur le champ.* Editions Sagesse, Paris.

1936 *Ramures.* Editions G.L.M., Paris.

1937 *Vigies.* Editions G.L.M., Paris.

    1962 Second edition. Editions Alexandre Loewy, Paris.

1938 *La deuxième aventure céleste de Monsieur Antipyrine.* Editions des Réverbères, Paris.

1939 *Midis gagnés.* Editions Denoel, Paris.

1948   Second augmented edition. Editions Denoel, Paris. (1939 text
         augmented with the collected *La main passe.*)

1944   *Ça va.* Centre des Intellectuels, Cahors.

1944   *Une route seul soleil.* Bibliothèque Française, Comité National des Ecrivains,
         Centre des Intellectuels, Toulouse.

1946   *Entre-temps.* Collection le Calligraphe (no. 4), Editions Le Point du Jour,
         Paris.

1946   *Le signe de vie.* Editions Bordas, Paris.

1946   *Terre sur terre.* Editions des Trois Collines, Geneva / Paris.

1947   *Morceaux choisis.* Editions Bordas, Paris.

1949   *Phases.* Collection Poésie 49, no. 13, Editions Seghers, Paris.

1949   *Sans coup férir.* Jean Aubier, Paris.

1950   *De mémoire d'homme.* Editions Bordas, Paris.

1950   *Parler seul.* Editions A. Maeght, Paris.

         1955   Second edition. Collection Planètes, no. 2, Editions Caractères,
                  Paris.

1951   *Le poids du monde.* Editions Au Colporteur, no. 5, Saint-Girons (Ariège).

1953   *La face intérieure.* Editions Seghers, Paris.

1955   *A haute flamme.* Printed by Raymond Jacquet, Paris.

1955   *La bonne heure.* Printed by Raymond Jacquet, Paris.

1955   *Miennes.* Editions Caractères, Paris.

1955   *Le temps naissant.* Editions P.A.B., Alès.

1956   *Le fruit permis.* Editions Caractères, Paris.

1957   *Frère bois.* Editions P.A.B., Alès.

1958   *La rose et le chien.* Editions P.A.B., Alès.

1961   *De la coupe aux lèvres. Choix de poèmes,* 1939–1961. 'Colosseo' series, no. 3,
         Edizioni Rapporti Europei, Rome.

1961   *Juste présent.* Collection La Rose des Vents, no. 3, Editions La Rose des
         Vents, Lausanne.

Other Writings

1924   *Sept manifestes Dada.* Editions du Diorama, Editions Jean Budry, Paris.

   1963   *Sept manifestes Dada, Lampisteries.* Jean-Jacques Pauvert, Paris. (1924
            text and a selection of Tzara's critical articles titled *Lampisteries.*)

   1968   *Les manifestes Dada: Sept manifestes Dada.* Libertés nouvelles, no. 1,
            Jean-Jacques Pauvert, Paris. (1924 text.)

1924   *Mouchoir de nuages. Tragédie en quinze actes.* Editions Sélection, Anvers.

1935   *Grains et issues.* Editions Denoel et Steele, Paris.

1946   *Le coeur à gaz* (play). Edition G.L.M., Paris.

1947   *La fuite. Poème dramatique en quatre actes et un épilogue.* Editions Gallimard, Paris.

1947   *Le surréalisme et l'après-guerre.* Editions Nagel, Paris.

1951   *L'Art Océanien.* Editions A.P.A.M., Paris.

1953   *Picasso et la poésie.* De Luca, Rome.

1954   *L'Egypte face à face.* Collection La Guilde du Livre, no. 207, Editions de Clairefontaine, Lausanne.

Oeuvres complètes

Edited and annotated by Henri Béhar. Flammarion, Paris.

Vol. 1: 1912–24. publ. 1975.

Vol. 2: 1925–33. publ. 1977.

Vol. 3: 1934–46. publ. 1979.

Vol. 4: 1947–63. publ. 1981.

Vol. 5: *Les ecluses de la poèsie.* Appendices. publ. 1982.

Note: A much-expanded Tzara bibliography prepared by Lee Harwood was published by Aloes Books, London, 1974. The full bibliography lists complete details of each book of Tristan Tzara's work published between 1916 and 1968, joint publications, prefaces by Tzara, magazines including his work, translations of his work published between 1922 and 1971, and critical studies.

Acknowledgements

The majority of these poems were first published by Trigram Press (London) in 1975. The collection was titled *Tristan Tzara: Selected Poems*. A revised and augmented second edition was later published by Coach House Press / Underwhich Editions (Toronto) in 1987 and titled *Chanson Dada: Tristan Tzara Selected Poems*. Previously some of the poems had appeared in the magazines *Ant's Forefoot, Eleventh Finger, Flame, Frice, Juillard, Night Scene, Night Train, Oleo, Pennsylvania Review, Poetmeat, Poetry Review* (London), *Soho, Tzarad,* and in the pamphlets "Tristan Tzara—Cosmic Realities…: A poem sequence" (ARC Publications, 1969; 2nd rev. edn. 1975) and "Tristan Tzara—Destroyed Days" (Voiceprint Editions, 1971). The essay "Dada / my heart belongs to dada" was published in the *South-East Arts Review* (England), issue 17, spring 1981. This essay has been slightly revised for this present edition.

My thanks to these publishers and editors, and especially Asa Benveniste of Trigram Press and bpNichol of Underwhich Editions.

L. H.

A Life of Poems, Poems of a Life by Anna de Noailles. Translated by Norman R. Shapiro. Introduction by Catherine Perry.

Approximate Man and Other Writings by Tristan Tzara. Translated and edited by Mary Ann Caws.

Art Poétique by Guillevic. Translated by Maureen Smith.

The Big Game by Benjamin Péret. Translated with an introduction by Marilyn Kallet.

Boris Vian Invents Boris Vian: A Boris Vian Reader. Edited and translated by Julia Older.

Capital of Pain by Paul Eluard. Translated by Mary Ann Caws, Patricia Terry, and Nancy Kline.

Chanson Dada: Selected Poems by Tristan Tzara. Translated with an introduction and essay by Lee Harwood.

Essential Poems and Writings of Joyce Mansour: A Bilingual Anthology. Translated with an introduction by Serge Gavronsky.

Essential Poems and Prose of Jules Laforgue. Translated and edited by Patricia Terry.

Essential Poems and Writings of Robert Desnos: A Bilingual Anthology. Edited with an introduction and essay by Mary Ann Caws.

EyeSeas (Les Ziaux) by Raymond Queneau. Translated with an introduction by Daniela Hurezanu and Stephen Kessler.

Fables in a Modern Key by Pierre Coran. Edited and translated by Norman R. Shapiro. Full-color illustrations by Olga Pastuchiv.

Forbidden Pleasures: New Selected Poems 1924–1949 by Luis Cernuda. Translated by Stephen Kessler.

Furor and Mystery & Other Writings by René Char. Edited and translated by Mary Ann Caws and Nancy Kline.

The Gentle Genius of Cécile Périn: Selected Poems (1906–1956). Edited and translated by Norman R. Shapiro.

Guarding the Air: Selected Poems of Gunnar Harding. Translated and edited by Roger Greenwald.

The Inventor of Love & Other Writings by Gherasim Luca. Translated by Julian & Laura Semilian. Introduction by Andrei Codrescu. Essay by Petre Răileanu.

Jules Supervielle: Selected Prose and Poetry. Translated by Nancy Kline and Patricia Terry.

La Fontaine's Bawdy by Jean de La Fontaine. Translated with an introduction by Norman R. Shapiro. Illustrated by David Schorr.

Last Love Poems of Paul Eluard. Translated with an introduction by Marilyn Kallet.

Love, Poetry (L'amour la poésie) by Paul Eluard. Translated with an essay by Stuart Kendall.

Pierre Reverdy: Poems, Early to Late. Translated by Mary Ann Caws and Patricia Terry.

Poems of André Breton: A Bilingual Anthology. Translated with essays by Jean-Pierre Cauvin and Mary Ann Caws.

Poems of A. O. Barnabooth by Valery Larbaud. Translated by Ron Padgett and Bill Zavatsky.

Poems of Consummation by Vicente Aleixandre. Translated by Stephen Kessler.

Préversities: A Jacques Prévert Sampler. Translated and edited by Norman R. Shapiro.

The Sea and Other Poems by Guillevic. Translated by Patricia Terry. Introduction by Monique Chefdor.

To Speak, to Tell You? Poems by Sabine Sicaud. Translated by Norman R. Shapiro. Introduction and notes by Odile Ayral-Clause.

Forthcoming Translations

Earthlight (Clair de Terre) by André Breton. Translated by Bill Zavatsky and Zack Rogrow. (New and revised edition.)

Fables of Town and Country by Pierre Coran. Translated by Norman R. Shapiro. Full-color illustrations by Olga Pastuchiv.

MODERN POETRY SERIES

ABC of Translation by Willis Barnstone

An Alchemist with One Eye on Fire
by Clayton Eshleman

An American Unconscious by Mebane Robertson

Anticline by Clayton Eshleman

Archaic Design by Clayton Eshleman

Backscatter: New and Selected Poems
by John Olson

Barzakh (Poems 2000–2012) by Pierre Joris

The Caveat Onus by Dave Brinks

City Without People: The Katrina Poems
by Niyi Osundare

*Clayton Eshleman/The Essential Poetry:
1960–2015*

Concealments and Caprichos
by Jerome Rothenberg

Crusader-Woman
by Ruxandra Cesereanu. Translated by Adam J.
Sorkin. Introduction by Andrei Codrescu.

Curdled Skulls: Poems of Bernard Bador. Translated
by Bernard Bador with Clayton Eshleman.

Disenchanted City (La ville désenchantée)
by Chantal Bizzini. Translated by J. Bradford
Anderson, Darren Jackson, and Marilyn Kallet.

Endure: Poems by Bei Dao.
Translated by Clayton Eshleman and Lucas Klein.

Exile Is My Trade: A Habib Tengour Reader.
Translated by Pierre Joris.

Eye of Witness: A Jerome Rothenberg Reader.
Edited with commentaries by Heriberto Yepez
& Jerome Rothenberg.

Fire Exit by Robert Kelly

Forgiven Submarine
by Ruxandra Cesereanu and Andrei Codrescu

from stone this running by Heller Levinson

Grindstone of Rapport: A Clayton Eshleman Reader

The Hexagon by Robert Kelly

Larynx Galaxy by John Olson

The Love That Moves Me by Marilyn Kallet

Memory Wing by Bill Lavender

Packing Light: New and Selected Poems
by Marilyn Kallet

The Present Tense of the World: Poems 2000–2009
by Amina Saïd. Translated with an introduction
by Marilyn Hacker.

The Price of Experience by Clayton Eshleman

The Secret Brain: Selected Poems 1995–2012
by Dave Brinks

Signal from Draco: New and Selected Poems
by Mebane Robertson

Soraya (Sonnets) by Anis Shivani

Wrack Lariat by Heller Levinson

Forthcoming Modern Poetry Titles

Dada Budapest by John Olson

Fractal Song by Jerry Ward

Funny Way of Staying Alive by Willis Barnstone

Memory by Bernadette Mayer

Geometry of Sound by Dave Brinks

Penetralia by Clayton Eshleman

LITERARY THEORY /
BIOGRAPHY SERIES

*Barbaric Vast & Wild: A Gathering of Outside and
Subterranean Poetry (Poems for the Millennium,
vol. 5).* Eds: Jerome Rothenberg and John
Bloomberg-Rissman

Clayton Eshleman: The Whole Art
by Stuart Kendall

Revolution of the Mind: The Life of André Breton
by Mark Polizzotti